SEMINAR STUDIES IN HISTORY

General Editor: Roger Lockyer

The Attlee Governments 1945–1951

Kevin Jefferys

Senior Lecturer in History,
Polytechnic South West

LONGMAN

and New York

Longman Group UK Limited,
Longman House, Burnt Mill, Harlow,
Essex CM20 2JE, England
and Associated Companies throughout the world.

Published in the United States of America
by Longman Inc., New York.

First published 1992
Third impression 1994

Set in 10/11 point Baskerville (Linotron)
Produced through Longman Malaysia, PA

ISBN 0 582 061059

British Library Cataloguing in Publication Data
Jefferys, Kevin, *1959–*
    The Attlee governments, 1945–51. – (Seminar studies in history)
    I. Title   II. Series
    354.410009

    ISBN 0-582-06105-9

Library of Congress Cataloging-in-Publication Data
Jefferys, Kevin.
    The Attlee governments, 1945–1951 / Kevin Jefferys.
        p.   cm. – (Seminar studies in history)
    Includes bibliographical references and index.
    ISBN 0-582-06105-9:
    1. Great Britain – Politics and government – 1945–1964.   2. Attlee,
C. R. (Clement Richard), 1883–1967.   3. Labour Party (Great Britain)
I. Title.   II. Series.
    DA588.J44   1992
    941.085'4 – dc20   91–30809
                                                                         CIP

Contents

Acknowledgements

I should like to dedicate this book to my parents, for all their support and encouragement.

K. J.

We are grateful to the following for permission to reproduce copyright material:

Authors' Agents for extracts from *High Tide and After: Memoirs* by Hugh Dalton, pubd. Frederick Muller; Authors' Agents on behalf of Nuffield College/Random Century Group on behalf of Jonathan Cape as publishers, for extracts from *The Diary of Hugh Gaitskill* edited by P. Williams; Victor Gollancz Ltd for an extract from *I've Lived Through It All* by Emanuel Shinwell; the Controller of Her Majesty's Stationery Office for an extract from *Documents on British Policy Overseas* 1, III. ed. R. Bullen & M. Pelly; Authors' Agents for extracts from *Change and Fortune* by Douglas Jay, pubd. Hutchinson; Labour Party Sales for an extract from *The Labour Party Election Manifestos* 1945 & 1950; Random Century Group for extracts from *The Political Diary of Hugh Dalton* 1915–40, 1945–60 by Dr. Ben Pimlott, pubd. Jonathan Cape; The Royal Institute of International Affairs for an extract from *Documents and Speeches on Commonwealth Affairs* 1931–52, Vol II. ed. N. Mansergh, pubd. by Oxford University Press for the Royal Institute of International Affairs; Tribune Publications Ltd for an extract from *Tribune* 20.4.51.

We have unfortunately been unable to trace the copyright holders of *The Robert Hall Diaries* by A. Cairncross, and would appreciate any information which would enable us to do so.

Cover: Photograph of Clement Attlee chatting to a young supporter while touring his Walthamstow constituency on the morning of the general election of 23 February 1950. Photo: Topham Picture Source.

Seminar Studies in History
Founding Editor: Patrick Richardson

Introduction

The Seminar Studies series was conceived by Patrick Richardson, whose experience of teaching history persuaded him of the need for something more substantial than a textbook chapter but less formidable than the specialised full-length academic work. He was also convinced that such studies, although limited in length, should provide an up-to-date and authoritative introduction to the topic under discussion as well as a selection of relevant documents and a comprehensive bibliography.

Patrick Richardson died in 1979, but by that time the Seminar Studies series was firmly established, and it continues to fulfil the role he intended for it. This book, like others in the series, is therefore a living tribute to a gifted and original teacher.

Note on the System of References:
A bold number in round brackets (**5**) in the text refers the reader to the corresponding entry in the Bibliography section at the end of the book. A bold number in square brackets, preceded by 'doc.' [**doc. 6**] refers the reader to the corresponding item in the section of Documents, which follows the main text. A word followed by an asterisk, for example, 'Blitz*', indicates that the term is defined in the Glossary.

ROGER LOCKYER
General Editor

Foreword

The Attlee governments changed the face of Britain. After sweeping to power at the end of the Second World War, the Labour administration of 1945–50 presided over a series of far-reaching policy reforms, both at home and abroad. In domestic politics, attention focused on the introduction of a mixed economy and the welfare state. Within two years of its 1945 election success, Labour had secured major adjustments to the nation's pre-war, private-enterprise economy, avoiding any return to mass unemployment and forging ahead with an extensive programme of public ownership. At the same time, legislation had reached the statute book confirming the establishment of both a national health service and a new system of social security, designed to provide protection for all 'from the cradle to the grave'. By the time Attlee's second, short-lived government of 1950–51 left office, Labour could claim credit for the creation of a new order: a 'post-war settlement' that was to dominate domestic politics for a generation to come. In overseas policy, the legacy of these years was equally significant. British withdrawal from India was to mark the first stage in a transition from Empire to Commonwealth. And with the onset of the Cold War between the new superpowers, the United States and the Soviet Union, Labour's Foreign Secretary, Ernest Bevin, was instrumental in reshaping international affairs. Above all, as the 'iron curtain' descended across Europe, he played a pivotal role in cementing Britain's wartime alliance with the Americans, most notably through the creation of the North Atlantic Treaty Organisation. Abroad, as much as at home, these were changes that helped to set a pattern for subsequent decades.

Few would therefore deny that the Attlee governments were amongst the most formative in modern British history. But assessments of the outcome have been varied. Indeed in recent years, Labour's record in office has become the subject of increasing controversy, both among politicians and historians. During the 1980s, Conservative administrations under Mrs Thatcher consciously sought to break with much of the domestic post-war settlement. As a result, the 1945 government has been depicted on the political right as a wrong turning – a time when the powers of the state were unnecessarily extended, thereby undermining individual initiative and creating levels of social provision that would be unsustainable in the long term (**9**). For writers such as Corelli Barnett, concerned to explain the nation's relative industrial decline since the war, the 1940s were a decade when welfare reform was given an unwarranted priority over economic regeneration; a choice that was to ensure that the 'dreams of 1945 . . . turned to a dank reality of a segregated, subliterate, unskilled, unhealthy and institutionalised proletariat hanging on to the nipple of state maternalism' (**40**). The most detailed research on the Attlee governments, however, has been carried out by historians of the left. For some, such as Kenneth Morgan and Henry Pelling, the post-war period witnessed the most successful example yet of democratic socialism in practice. According to Morgan, the achievements of these years brought the Labour movement 'to the zenith of its achievement as a political instrument for humanitarian reform', and made the 1945 administration 'amongst the most effective of any British government since the passage of the 1832 Reform Act' (**20, 24**). Others have been less generous. Many left-wing critics see the period as one of wasted opportunity. Instead of thorough-going socialism, Labour offered only cautious change at home, involving little redistribution of wealth, and a foreign policy that tied Britain to the militantly capitalist United States (**10, 18, 27, 30**).

How then should the performance of the Attlee governments be judged? The aim of this study is to provide a brief overview of the major elements of Labour policy, and to make accessible a selection of the ever-increasing volume of relevant source material. The book begins by looking at the evolution of the Labour Party on the 'road to 1945', as well as introducing the key individuals who were to dominate the post-war years. This is followed by a consideration of several sub-debates crucial to a wider assessment of Labour's record. How far, for example, was domestic reform during 1945–46 the product of a distinct ideology, as opposed to the simple working-through of agreed wartime reforms? To what extent was the government's sense of direction undermined by recurrent economic crises in 1947? In what ways might Bevin as Foreign Secretary be accused of betraying hopes of a 'socialist foreign policy'? How far did the age of austerity associated with Chancellor Stafford Cripps mark a retreat towards consensus politics? Why did Labour finally fall from power in 1951, and with what consequence? The general argument of the study, implicit throughout, is spelt out more fully in the concluding chapter. While conceding the force of individual criticisms, Labour's overall performance, it will be claimed here, was one of unprecedented success. When set against the standard of previous twentieth-century governments, and in view of the legacy left by six years of total war, the 1945 administration could boast two overriding achievements: at home it created a more tolerable society, and abroad it made Britain more secure as an international power. In the words of the Prime Minister – not a man prone to exaggeration – this was to constitute a 'revolution without tears' (**85**, **106**).

Part One: The Background

1 Labour and the Road to 1945

The Labour Party came of age in 1945. As the Second World War drew to a close in Europe, the coalition government* of Conservative and Labour forces which had governed Britain since 1940 broke apart. Winston Churchill, the nation's inspirational wartime Prime Minister, now called upon the electorate to return him as the head of a new Conservative administration; he alone, Churchill claimed, was capable of dealing with the domestic and international legacy left by six years of war against Nazi Germany. Among politicians and commentators, it was widely anticipated that Churchill would sweep back to power in the general election of July 1945, just as Lloyd George had triumphed in 1918 as 'the man who won the war'. But this prediction proved to be wildly inaccurate. As the election results filtered through, it became apparent that the Labour Party had won a landslide victory. At the last pre-war election, held in 1935, Labour had trailed the Tory-dominated National government* by more than 200 parliamentary seats. In 1945, however, Labour secured nearly half the popular vote, winning 393 seats, compared with 210 for the Conservatives. On an average swing of 12 per cent, Labour made sweeping gains in towns and cities across the nation, capturing scores of constituencies that had never before returned a Labour member to the House of Commons. Hence it was not Churchill but the relatively unknown Labour leader, Clement Attlee, who went to Buckingham Palace to accept an invitation from the King to form Britain's post-war government (**16**). The war years had clearly wrought a remarkable political transformation. 'We', one Labour MP was reputed to have shouted at his opponents across the floor of the Commons chamber, 'are the masters now' (**32**).

But the road to 1945 – and the formation of the first-ever majority Labour government – had been long and arduous. Labour had only emerged as a distinct political force around the turn of the century, and for many years made little impression on the two dominant groups in Edwardian politics, the Conservatives and the Liberal Party. Before the First World War, the Labour Party, as it officially became known in 1906, was primarily a working-class pressure group. In an effort to protect workers' interests by securing greater parliamentary representation, leading trade unionists decided to ally themselves with socialist societies such as the Independent Labour Party*. It was in the latter that many senior ministers in the 1945 government, including Attlee, began their political careers. Historians have long been divided over the extent to which the rise of Labour can be traced back before 1914, though it is generally agreed that the new Labour alliance – of socialists and trade unionists – faced many teething problems. In competing for votes under the restricted pre-war franchise, any limited parliamentary successes were the product of electoral agreements with the Liberals, and the small band of Labour MPs at Westminster were distinguishable from progressive Liberals more in terms of social background than political philosophy. On the other hand, the seeds of future Labour success could be seen in rapidly growing trade-union support, bringing greatly increased financial resources and a growing identification of Labour as the natural party of the working classes (**15**).

The Great War led to a critical breakthrough for Labour. Asquith's Liberal government came under increasing strain in meeting the demands of total war, and gradually after 1916 Liberal forces became polarised between followers of Asquith and his replacement as Prime Minister, Lloyd George. The carnage on the Western front* placed immense strain on all the political parties, but building from a lower base Labour was suddenly presented with new possibilities. In 1918 a new constitution and organisational structure was adopted; from now on, Labour was pledged in theory to 'Clause Four Socialism'*, although in practice most party supporters remained wedded to a 'labourist' ideology, emphasising collectivist social change rather than outright rejection of capitalism. Above all, the 1918 constitution was a symbolic reflection of Labour's new-found confidence. With the Liberals in disarray, the party was well placed to benefit from a massive extension of the franchise after the war, and finally severed any lingering electoral ties with local Liberal forces. The strength of the Labour Party, as it had been before the war, was still confined to the industrial heartlands of Britain – in northern England, Scotland and Wales – but by the early 1920s Liberalism had lost its claim to be the established party of the left in British politics. In 1924 the arrival of a new force in national politics was confirmed when Ramsay MacDonald went to Downing Street to form the first Labour government (**17**).

The experience of 1924 was not, however, a happy one. As head of a minority administration, dependent upon Liberal support in the

House of Commons, MacDonald had few ambitions beyond demonstrating that Labour was 'fit to govern'. In terms of electoral strategy and party organisation, MacDonald proved an effective leader, but the first Labour government had little to show in the way of legislative success before a fresh election returned the Conservatives to power. Nor did MacDonald fare any better in domestic policy when Labour increased its share of the vote sufficiently to form a second minority government in 1929. The paucity of serious party thinking on economic issues was now exposed as a severe recession took hold, deepened by the effects of the Wall Street crash* in the United States. Labour's cautious and economically orthodox Chancellor, Philip Snowden, was powerless to prevent a steep rise in unemployment, and in 1931 the Cabinet split openly over proposed cuts in unemployment benefit. MacDonald defected to form a new 'National' government*, including Conservatives and many Liberals, leaving his former colleagues to stand condemned for their handling of the economic crisis. In the subsequent general election, the party was reduced to a rump of only some fifty MPs. The crisis of 1931 subsequently entered Labour mythology as the year of MacDonald's 'betrayal'; at the same time, it had cruelly highlighted the limitations of the formative Labour movement, both in terms of a lack of imaginative leadership and a failure to devise coherent and sustainable policies (**33**).

But the débâcle of 1931 did, in the longer term, open up a new phase in the party's history. Against the backcloth of the 'hungry thirties', it seemed for a while that Labour might move towards advocacy of direct attacks on the capitalist system. Pressure from the grass roots was channelled through a new organisation, the Socialist League, and the party's annual conference in the early 1930s resounded to calls for wholesale central planning and restrictions on bastions of the establishment such as the City of London. The challenge from the left, however, was gradually contained. Both the industrial and political wings of the movement continued to be dominated by men of less militant persuasion. Trade-union leaders, notably the powerful head of the Transport Workers, Ernest Bevin, on the whole had little sympathy with the radical demands of the Socialist League. The Parliamentary Labour Party (PLP) also came increasingly under the control of centrist figures such as Arthur Greenwood and Herbert Morrison, Labour leader of the London County Council. Although Attlee was regarded initially as a stop-gap figure, part of the reason for his emergence as leader of the PLP in 1935 was that he shared a broad concern with pragmatic reform, rather than with what was widely seen as the rhetorical and unworkable theories of the left. The emergence of an Attlee–Bevin axis at the top of the Labour movement, which was to continue for the next generation, produced some immediate effects. The party quickly rebuilt itself in industrial Britain and was able at the 1935 general election to recover much lost ground, though without seriously challenging the ascendancy of the National government* (**26**).

The new leadership also presided over a gradual redefinition of Labour policy. One of the lessons of 1931 for the party leadership was that the electorate would never again be convinced by the old-style rhetoric of MacDonald and Snowden. In its place, a talented group of Labour economists, guided by the former academic Hugh Dalton, evolved a new form of democratic socialism which combined demand management* with physical control economic planning*. The result was *Labour's Immediate Programme* of 1937, a pragmatic and radical policy document which called for wide-ranging state intervention to tackle unemployment, together with proposals for social reform that went far beyond prevailing Conservative practice. This domestic rethink – foreshadowing much of Labour's policy in office after 1945 – was also accompanied by a new realism in foreign policy. After Hitler's rise to power in Germany, the Labour movement gradually moved away from its traditional commitment to neo-pacifism* and abhorrence of 'capitalist war'. The party became increasingly hostile to the appeasement of the fascist dictators practised by the leader of the National government* after 1937, Neville Chamberlain. Although personal antipathy towards Chamberlain led Labour leaders to decline his offer of coalition once war had broken out, there was no doubt that Labour followers throughout the country would support the fight against Nazism (**26, 101**).

By September 1939 the Labour Party thus looked to have become once more a credible party of government. But there were as yet few signs that the electorate had lost faith in Chamberlain's National government. The experience of the Second World War changed all this, and provided the backcloth to the landslide victory of 1945. After Chamberlain fell from power in May 1940 – the result of frustration with early British setbacks in the war – there was a pronounced swing to the left in public opinion, though this was masked at the time by the suspension of normal political activity and by Churchill's immense popularity as war leader. The movement of public opinion began, following Britain's humiliating evacuation from Dunkirk, as a reaction against the so-called 'guilty men': Conservative leaders such as Chamberlain were accused of enabling Hitler to stand so menacingly across the Channel by mid-1940. More important as the war progressed was the egalitarian ethic which followed on from mobilisation of the entire civilian population and from the intense physical dangers of life in the Blitz*. If the Great War of 1914–18 had been fought for King and Country, then the conflict against Hitler soon came to be seen as a 'People's War' (**5**). After the 'turn of the tide' late in 1942, when the defeat of Nazism could for the first time be seriously contemplated, Labour also benefited from a sudden awakening of interest in welfare reform. Indicators of public feeling now showed a marked anti-Conservative trend, exacerbated by the Prime Minister's cool response to the Beveridge Report* on social security and other proposals for social change (**1**). By concentrating so exclusively on the war effort, Churchill clearly misjudged the desire of the British people to create a New Jerusalem – a theme made central in Labour's electoral propaganda at the end of the war [**doc. 1**]. Only the Labour Party, it now seemed, could offer both immediate redress for a war-weary population and a long-term commitment to a reconstructed, welfare state. As David Howell has written: '"bread and butter plus a dream". That was the secret of 1945' (**12**).

The war years also produced some further refinements in Labour policy. Traditionally, historians have claimed that the war created a new 'middle ground' upon which all political parties would henceforth compete for power. Paul Addison in particular has argued that in contrast to the negative hostility of the inter-war years, there suddenly emerged between Conservative and Labour forces a common commitment to social reform, a new 'consensus' which foreshadowed an era of much closer party co-operation after 1945 (**1**). Without doubt, the atmosphere of a 'People's War' generated immense pressure for the creation of a brave new world, but how far this amounted to a new political consensus remains open to question. The coalition's reconstruction programme, some historians have argued, never proceeded very far in practice because of intractable ideological differences between the main parties. Mainstream Conservative opinion, following Churchill's lead, continued to have grave doubts about the cost and desirability of greatly enhancing state activity. The welfare state and the mixed economy*, in other words, were not inevitable products of the Second World War, but derived to a greater extent from Labour's democratic socialist tradition as it emerged and developed after 1931 (**14**). Much of Labour's programme, such as its commitment to nationalisation, became more acceptable during the war years when the public became accustomed to wholesale planning of the economy. At the same time, partnership in Churchill's coalition, though uncomfortable for many party activists, allowed Labour leaders such as Attlee, Bevin and Morrison to demonstrate their ministerial capabilities. This schooling in the hard realities of high office, combined with the sharpening of party policy and the popular enthusiasm shown at the polls in 1945, enabled Attlee to come to power in circumstances markedly different from those that attended the earlier MacDonald administrations. At the end of the Second World War, Labour had not simply swept to power; for the first time in its history, the party was ready to use it.

2   Into Power

News of Labour's electoral victory occasioned much surprise. Most commentators had assumed that Churchill would remain in power, and even seasoned Labour campaigners were slightly bemused as the scale of the party's landslide became apparent [**doc. 2**]. Fifteen minutes after Churchill left Buckingham Palace in his chauffeur-driven Rolls-Royce on the evening of 26 July, Mr and Mrs Attlee arrived in their Standard 10 looking, according to the King, 'very surprised indeed' at the turn of events (**105**). After accepting the royal invitation to form a government, Attlee left to prepare for office amidst noisy cheering and singing, though his assumption of power was not quite as untroubled as it seemed. Earlier in the day, Herbert Morrison – who had unsuccessfully challenged for the leadership back in 1935 – claimed that under party rules an administration could not be formed before the PLP had given its approval. With the backing of Ernest Bevin, Attlee met this challenge as he was to meet many in the future: he ignored it (**20, 24**). These manoeuvres behind the scenes were not allowed to spoil the party's victory celebrations, and indeed in some ways Morrison's challenge was deceptive. For unlike MacDonald's experience in the 1920s, the Attlee years were – with a few important exceptions – to be characterised by strong leadership and by a high degree of unity at all levels of the Labour movement. Almost immediately after becoming Prime Minister, Attlee left to discuss post-war problems at the Potsdam Conference*, returning now as Britain's official representative, rather than at Churchill's invitation as before. But before leaving, Attlee made sure that the nucleus of his Cabinet team was in place. Within twenty-four hours of the election result, in fact, press commentators were already noting the existence of Labour's 'big five'; a group of senior ministers who were to dominate British politics for the next five years.

Herbert Morrison was not alone in doubting the abilities of the new Prime Minister. Several of his contemporaries, and historians in turn, have found it difficult to explain how the aloof, enigmatic Clement Attlee – 'Clem the Clam', as the King called him – could prevail over his colleagues throughout these years. He was, according to some critics, a 'modest man with much to be modest about'; or, at best, 'a good mayor of Stepney in a bad year': a reference to the London borough where Attlee had established himself in Labour politics after 1918. On the 'equivalent of the Richter scale for oratory', notes Peter Hennessy, 'the needle scarcely flickered' (**9**), and there was no doubt that Attlee's terse style made him a difficult, at times unnerving, colleague. One junior minister found himself summoned to Downing Street, thinking he was to be congratulated on the work of his department. 'What can I do for you, Prime Minister?' he asked. 'I want your job,' Attlee replied. The minister was stunned. 'But . . . why, Prime Minister?' he enquired. 'Afraid you're not up to it,' Attlee said, concluding the interview (**95**). What this incident also illustrated, however, was Attlee's considerable self-confidence, the product of his middle-class background and public-school training. He might, Kenneth Morgan writes, more accurately be described as 'an immodest little man with plenty to be immodest about' (**21**). Certainly Attlee's confidence grew after 1945 as he showed himself to be an effective co-ordinator of government policy. He conducted Cabinet affairs briskly, without the rambling diversions of Churchill's leadership, and with the exception of events in 1947, he commanded loyalty from Cabinet colleagues. As for the Labour movement as a whole, Attlee may have lacked MacDonald's charisma, but this was seen to be no bad thing, and it was more than made up for by integrity and loyalty to the party's major policy aims. Whatever his shortcomings, none of Attlee's colleagues were equipped in the same way for the unique demands of the premiership [**doc. 3**].

The Prime Minister's closest colleague was Ernest Bevin. In the aftermath of the election, Bevin was marked down as an obvious choice for the Treasury. His reputation had been built around industrial and economic expertise, initially as Britain's most powerful trade-union leader between the wars, and then as Minister of Labour in the wartime coalition, where he played a vital role in mobilising the civilian population. For a variety of reasons, including the desire to keep Bevin and Morrison in separate spheres of influence, Attlee decided that Bevin would be best suited to international rather than domestic affairs. In the next five years, he was to establish himself as 'a dockers' John Bull, a British Foreign Secretary of Chatham- or Palmerston-like proportions' (**21**). The irony here was that Bevin was far from being traditional Foreign Office material. The semi-literate son of a farm labourer, he was a man of 'fierce and often difficult temperament'; a no-nonsense figure who never sought to conceal his strong prejudices and who tended to ride roughshod over opponents of his policy (**84**). Bevin was, said one of his colleagues, possibly the toughest statesman Labour had yet produced; someone quite willing to give the Tories a good 'kick up the pants' whenever he deemed it necessary (**97**). With his massive physical presence, Bevin was in many respects the strongest personality in the 1945 government; his ability to influence the Cabinet on domestic, as well as foreign, affairs was one illustration of this. In spite of his egotism, however, he was never tempted by suggestions that he might displace the Prime Minister. Rather, Bevin and Attlee, both loners in their own ways, developed a relationship that was the closest either had in politics; it was this alliance that dominated Cabinet proceedings until 1950. Bevin's belief that loyalty was a prime political virtue helps to explain why he remained on such poor terms with the third member of Labour's inner cabinet, Herbert Morrison.

As the leading spirit behind the creation of the London Labour Party, Morrison has always been seen as the 'embodiment of the cockney spirit, chirpy, full of backchat'. He certainly continued to believe, as he had since 1935, that he would make a more effective, high-profile party leader than Attlee; and his preoccupation with internal party matters led many to dismiss Morrison as a machine politician, more interested in intrigue than high policy. He had, in the words of one of his opponents, 'nothing more than the mind of an election agent' (**21, 91**). Morrison's lack of scruple on occasion, and the antagonism he aroused as a result, have tended to overshadow the indispensable contribution that he made to the effectiveness of the 1945 government. Appointed as Lord President of the Council and Leader of the House of Commons, Morrison was in effect deputy Prime Minister, presiding over Cabinet whenever Attlee was absent. His primary function as a minister was to coordinate policy on the home front. In this context, the range of his responsibilities stretched from economic planning and nationalisation to consideration of the future legislative programme. Beyond this, Morrison was charged with maintaining the morale and unity of the parliamentary party, acting as a direct link between ministers and back-benchers. He was thus a 'political boss', but he was also much more. Morrison's ubiquitous presence meant he acted as a strong influence on both the policy and the organisation of the Labour Party after 1945; he was, in the words of one of his Conservative opponents, 'the Government's handyman' (**91**).

The two remaining members of the 'big five' had a profound impact on the fortunes of the Labour government, though for shorter periods of time. The Chancellor of the Exchequer from 1945 until the end of 1947 was Hugh Dalton, in many ways an underrated figure within the party hierarchy. In spite of his key role in redefining Labour policy during the 1930s, and notwithstanding a background that suited him for the Treasury – as an economist and wartime minister at the Board of Trade – there were still many critics of Dalton. Part of the reason for this was that his personality, as with Morrison's, tended to distort recognition of undoubted qualities. His loud and overbearing manner proved unsettling to friends and opponents alike. 'He curves his towering, six-foot-three inch frame far over the Dispatch Box', wrote one parliamentary observer, 'screws his bald domed head sideways and upwards and, from time to time, rolls his pale blue eyes so that the whites blaze and flash' (**101**). Dalton relished the gossip of everyday Westminster politics, and almost gloried in a reputation for intrigue, but at the same time he had clearly defined and consistent 'grounding principles'. His beliefs, one colleague noted, were 'beautifully simple and clear. He was in favour of miners, the young, white men, socialists, New Zealand, Australia and dwellers in Durham and Northumberland. He was against the Germans, reactionaries, the elderly and the rich' (**96**). These prejudices helped to guide Dalton as Chancellor after 1945. In the early months of the Labour government, as we shall see, it was Dalton who took the lead in shaping domestic policy, seeking to ensure above all the maintenance of a radical sense of purpose. By proclaiming his socialist faith 'with a song in his heart', and by taunting the opposition with deliberate insults, he became the most reviled senior minister amongst Conservatives. 'Keep that man away from me', Churchill would remark; 'I can't stand his booming voice and shifting eyes' (**21, 90**).

On a personal level, there could be no greater contrast than between Hugh Dalton and his successor as Chancellor, Sir Stafford Cripps. Where Dalton was exuberant and voluble, Cripps had a reputation for aloofness and austerity. A teetotaller and vegetarian, whose working day began with a cold bath at four in the morning, Cripps had an unconventional background in the Labour movement. He came from an affluent, upper-middle-class family, and had an established career in the legal profession before his intense religious conviction took him into politics. For many years, Cripps was regarded with suspicion by Labour leaders. He was closely identified with the 'extremism' of the left and expelled from the party in

1939. As an 'Independent Socialist' he became Britain's wartime ambassador to the Soviet Union, in which capacity Churchill described him as 'a lunatic in a country of lunatics' (**26**, **97**). After returning from Moscow in 1942, untainted by the failures of the coalition, Cripps for a while attracted widespread support and posed a challenge to Churchill's leadership. But the 'turn of the tide' reinforced the Prime Minister's popularity; Cripps was removed from the Cabinet and spent the remainder of the war as an efficient, if rather unnoticed, Minister of Aircraft Production (**89**). It was this experience, combined with ministerial responsibility at the Board of Trade after 1945, which convinced him that socialism must become wedded to productive efficiency and the modernisation of industry. By demonstrating firm resolve during the economic crises of 1947, Cripps was to emerge as the obvious successor to Dalton, and for the next three years he set the tone for the government's whole economic strategy. As other senior figures began to crack under the strain of high office, Cripps became an ever-more-dominant force, and Labour's prospects of re-election became inextricably linked with his efforts to combine 'hard-headedness' with 'warm-heartedness' (**21**).

The remaining ministers who sat around the Cabinet table, after Attlee's return from Potsdam, exercised varying degrees of influence, but without ever emulating the reputation of the 'big five'. About half of the Cabinet's twenty members were solid, loyal and experienced party stalwarts, such as Arthur Greenwood and James Chuter Ede, who was rewarded for his work as an Education Minister during the war with the post of Home Secretary (**97**). In line with the balance of party forces, Attlee appointed only a limited number of those on the Labour left. Emanuel (Manny) Shinwell and 'Red Ellen' Wilkinson had made their names as fiery radicals before the war, but both were to prove cautious and pragmatic ministers after 1945. This meant that the most prominent representative of the left in Cabinet was its youngest member, Aneurin ('Nye') Bevan, the outspoken MP for Ebbw Vale whose talents were used to full effect at the Ministry of Health. On various occasions over the next few years, Bevan was highly critical of what he saw as the unnecessary caution of Cabinet colleagues, though before his resignation over health-service cuts in 1951, he never seriously challenged the main thrust of the government's programme (**88**, **92**). Hence Attlee, unlike MacDonald before him, was blessed with a talented and united team, though one frequently accused of being elderly in composition. Outside the Cabinet in the government as a whole, only three new

11

members of the parliamentary party were rewarded with office in 1945, the youngest being Harold Wilson, a high-flying civil servant during the war who was now appointed as a junior minister at the Ministry of Works (**24**). Although it was understandable at the outset that Attlee should rely on those who had proved their competence in the wartime coalition, limited opportunities for promotion from the middle ranks brought with them frustrations and dangers. When Cripps retired as Chancellor, there were few serious contenders to replace him, and a generation was skipped in giving the post to Hugh Gaitskell, another of those who entered Parliament only in 1945. Gaitskell's inexperience, as we shall see, was one of the causes of the major party split that developed in 1951.

In the meantime, a strong and harmonious Cabinet had little trouble in controlling the various constituent parts of the Labour movement. The general quiescence of the parliamentary party at first sight appears surprising. The year 1945 had transformed the PLP, bringing in some 260 new back-benchers after the election. The House of Commons, complained one disgruntled Conservative, suddenly seemed to be filled with 'half-baked young men, mostly from the RAF' (**14**). Aside from having served in the war, the new Labour MPs were generally more middle-class and articulate than their pre-war counterparts, and yet there was to be little of the constant sniping against ministers that had so beset the MacDonald administrations. Part of the reason for this was organisational. Leaders such as Morrison went to considerable lengths to ensure that back-bench opinion was channelled in constructive directions. A special liaison committee was established to maintain contact between ministers and MPs; the party's standing orders were suspended, thereby allowing divergent expressions of opinion without fear of disciplinary action; and specialist subject groups were set up, enabling back-benchers to develop their own particular interests (**91**). Not all of these subject groups proved successful – Ernest Bevin complained that the foreign-affairs group contained 'every sort of freak harboured in our majority' – and indeed it would be wrong to assume that the Attlee years were free from parliamentary dissent. Five MPs were to be expelled from the party, mostly for publicly voicing pro-Soviet views, and on nearly forty separate occasions Labour MPs attacked aspects of government policy. But there was little sustained or co-ordinated opposition. The so-called 'Keep Left' group* of 1946–47 saw itself as being constructively critical, and with different sets of MPs voicing doubts on particular topics, ministers could comfort themselves that the government's large majority was never seriously endangered (**20**, **31**). Apart from the imperatives of party management, this record of harmony reflected a broad approval of Cabinet leadership by back-benchers; Attlee was later to describe the 1945 Parliament as the most loyal he could remember (**2**).

The same loyalty was characteristic of Labour politics outside the confines of Westminster. At the party's annual conference, which remained under the 1918 constitution a major instrument in policy formation – at least in theory – ministers did occasionally suffer defeat. But such setbacks were usually on minor topics, and produced no alteration in the direction of government policy. Although critics used the conference platform to voice concerns, notably over foreign affairs, the general tone of proceedings was placid: the year 1946 saw a 'victory parade', and by 1949 the prospect of a forthcoming election served to reinforce the need for unity. Labour's rank-and-file, therefore, followed the lead of the PLP in throwing its weight behind the government. Criticism from the constituencies was to build up after 1950, though again without reaching proportions worrying for ministers (**31**, **35**). Part of the reason why support could be so effectively mobilised in the country was the benign attitude of the industrial wing of the Labour movement. The proportion of trade-union-sponsored MPs had fallen sharply: from 51 per cent of the PLP in 1935 to 31 per cent in 1945 (**24**). But the political–industrial alliance remained critical for Labour, and Attlee sought to ensure that leading trade unionists were represented at the highest levels of the party. He could also take comfort from the fact that major unions – such as the Transport Workers, the Miners, and the General and Municipal Workers – remained in the hands of moderate leaders, hostile to attempts at Communist infiltration on the shop-floor. Until 1950, when new strains began to emerge, the relationship between government and unions continued to be harmonious and effective.

The omens thus looked good for Attlee in the summer of 1945. He had assembled a talented team of ministers hardened by wartime experience, and came to power with a detailed programme enthusiastically endorsed by the electorate. The civil service, because of the war, had become accustomed to administering the type of interventionist policies favoured by Labour (**8**). Nor was there much to fear, at least in the short term, from the Conservative Party, demoralised by the election result and sunk for a while in recrimination. When the House of Commons reassembled, Tory MPs tried to lift themselves by greeting Churchill with a rendition of 'For he's a jolly good fellow', only to find that the crowded government benches responded with a rousing version of 'The red flag'. The sense of a new dawn in British politics was unmistakable. At the first two by-elections of the new Parliament, government candidates increased already large majorities, and in local elections during the autumn Labour swept the board, capturing seats that had been Conservative-controlled since the turn of the century (**6, 32**). The new Prime Minister also showed himself more adept at the despatch box than many expected, accusing Churchill, in their first major exchange, of personal responsibility for the election result. 'To the Right Hon. Gentleman everything that is Conservative is normal, anything that sees a changing world, and wishes to change it, must be wrong . . . . We were not returned for that purpose' (**95**). Labour's confidence in its ability to meet the demands of a changing world was, however, to be severely tested over the next five years. For if the Second World War had transformed the domestic political scene, it had also left Britain more clearly at the mercy of world events. Even as Attlee was completing the formation of his Cabinet, news came through that America had dropped atomic bombs* on Japan, thereby securing an unexpectedly early end to the war in the Far East and raising further questions about the nature of the new international order. After the euphoria of July 1945, it was not long before the question was being posed: would the new government's ambitious programme be undermined by circumstances beyond its control?

Part Two: Analysis – Labour in Office

3 Forging Britain's Post-war Settlement, 1945–46

The Labour government had no shortage of ambition. Hugh Dalton, newly installed as Chancellor, identified six urgent priorities: the reconversion to peaceful purposes of industry and manpower; the maintenance of high levels of employment while avoiding industrial unrest or inflation; honouring manifesto commitments on welfare reform; reducing onerous levels of wartime taxation; undertaking an extensive programme of nationalisation; and finally – a precondition of all else – finding ways for Britain to pay its way in world markets (**90**). But as Churchill had been well aware, and as Dalton and his colleagues soon discovered, the prospects for an ambitious post-war programme were overshadowed by one overriding problem: victory over Hitler had been achieved at enormous economic cost. During the course of the war years, Britain had lost almost a quarter of its entire national wealth. The national debt had increased threefold, and as the world's largest debtor nation in 1945, Britain had become heavily reliant upon the sale of overseas assets and the so-called 'Lend-Lease'* system of financial assistance from the United States. British exports had fallen by two-thirds as industry geared itself up for war production, and it was estimated that the volume of exports would have to be increased by 175 per cent simply to recover wartime losses; this at a time when raw materials were difficult to obtain and manpower shortages acute (**45**). The dire economic consequences of the war were compounded, moreover, by the sudden surrender of the Japanese. Within a week of the ending of hostilities in the Far East, President Truman abruptly terminated Lend-Lease*, thereby undermining British hopes for a lengthy transition from war to peace that would allow a much-needed breathing space. Lord Keynes, working as a special adviser at the Treasury, now told the Chancellor that Britain was facing a 'financial Dunkirk' [**doc. 4**].

The Cabinet's response to this crisis was to send Keynes to Washington in order to negotiate fresh terms with the United States.

Initially it was hoped that a generous, interest-free loan might be forthcoming. But the Americans proved themselves tough negotiators, suspicious of 'socialism' in Britain and 'imperialism' on the world stage. As the talks dragged on, the optimism of the British delegation was eroded, and Cabinet ministers found themselves flooded with telegrams requesting advice. 'The plethora of telegrams did not always make for clarity,' noted one observer. Dalton turned suddenly to Bevin at one stage to ask: '"Foreign Secretary, have you got the telegram?" "I've got 'undreds", replied Bevin' (**101, 102**). Eventually, in December 1945, the government accepted terms that seemed, at first sight, advantageous. Britain was offered a loan of 3.75 billion dollars (supplemented by an additional Canadian loan); repayment was to be spread over fifty years, and would not begin until 1951. But there were strings attached. In particular, ministers had to agree that sterling would become freely convertible into dollars after only a year. British negotiators had favoured a five-year transition period before multilateral trading arrangements were resumed, believing that any shorter time scale would place an intolerable strain on the British economy – a fear that was to be fully borne out in 1947. In the circumstances, however, the Cabinet, with only Bevan and Shinwell dissenting, believed there was no option but to acquiesce. To do otherwise, it was claimed, would mean accepting living standards lower even than in wartime. This argument was reluctantly accepted by the PLP, though a minority stood out against the implied subservience to American demands. Two factors above all swayed Labour opinion: in the first place, the direct political calculation that without the loan, biting austerity would be blamed on 'socialism'. There was, moreover, a recognition that convertibility was the price that had to be paid if the party was to have any prospect of fulfilling its most cherished ambition: the introduction of sweeping reforms on the home front (**101**).

Once the American loan had been secured, Attlee's Cabinet wasted no time in forging ahead to create a new domestic order: commonly referred to as the 'mixed economy'* and the 'welfare state'. Two particular questions arise about Labour's legislative and administrative programme. In the first place, how distinctive were the government's reforms after 1945? For many historians, the pressures of war had opened up a new era of co-operation or 'consensus' in British politics, with much greater agreement about the need for welfare reform; this consensus, it has been argued, 'fell like a branch of ripe plums into the lap of Mr Attlee' (**1, 54**). Others, however, have claimed that the war did not produce any fundamental convergence of opinion on domestic policy between the major parties, and that some – if not all – of Labour's programme after 1945 represented important departures from wartime orthodoxy (**14, 20**). The second main question concerns the impact and significance, as much as the origins, of the post-war settlement. To some sympathetic historians, this was a period when Labour achieved the maximum possible in testing circumstances, retaining throughout a clear vision of the need for radical change (**20, 24**). But left-wing critics bemoan the lack of fundamental restructuring in British society, claiming that these years produced only 'welfare capitalism', a compromise that betrayed the socialist ambitions of 1945 (**10, 30**). How then might the origins and significance of the post-war settlement be assessed?

In economic policy, the government's priorities were largely predetermined: without improved productivity and the recovery of export markets, welfare reforms would be impossible to realise. But from the outset Hugh Dalton, the Chancellor, was determined not to lose sight of broader objectives. Labour ministers were, he declared in November 1945,

> determined to advance along the road towards economic and social equality. We are not to be deflected by those Tory wiseacres, who tell us that complete equality is both unattainable and undesirable. That is not the point. As Jeremy Bentham once said, 'perfect equality is a chimera; all we can do is to diminish inequality'. And we mean to do that in this Parliament (**90**).

With this in mind, the Chancellor made concerted efforts to improve the lot of ordinary working people, the majority of whom were still suffering the hardships associated with rationing and war shortages. Food subsidies were maintained at high wartime levels in order to keep down living costs, and taxation structures were deliberately amended to benefit lower wage earners; Dalton's first two budgets took some 2.5 million workers out of the tax system altogether. These changes did not make the decisive impact upon poverty claimed by some at the time, and Britain's entrenched class structure remained stubbornly resistant to change. But the Chancellor's policies did reflect an unprecedented emphasis by central government on the redistribution of income – a factor attested to by the loud complaints from the Opposition, especially over increases in surtax and death duties (**101**).

Dalton was also determined to avoid the type of post-war slump that had so blighted working-class families after 1918. The aim of maintaining a 'high and stable level of employment' had earlier been embraced by the wartime coalition, though with little agreement as to how this might actually be achieved (**62**). Careful planning ensured that the most immediate obstacle was successfully overcome; within eighteen months millions of service personnel had been demobilised without any significant rise in unemployment, which remained at under 2 per cent of the working population. The government could be thankful for a revival of world trade which provided a much-needed boost to exports, but beyond this, Labour ministers brought with them into office some distinctive elements of policy. At the Board of Trade, for instance, Stafford Cripps introduced a vigorous approach to regional initiatives. This was made possible from the outset by the existence on the statute book of the 1945 Distribution of Industry Act – a measure to which Conservative industrialists had strongly objected (**14**). Such an approach helped to ensure that economic recovery rapidly spread to areas blighted in the 1930s, such as the industrial heartlands of northern England and the Welsh valleys, which now saw unprecedented levels of investment (**19**, **45**). This in turn was to have a lasting electoral legacy. Through all the economic difficulties that were to come before 1950, Labour's strongest claim on the loyalty of working-class voters was that it had become 'the party of full employment, the party which had exorcised the ghosts of Jarrow, Wigan and Merthyr Tydfil' – the most notorious of the inter-war blackspots (**20**).

The most distinctive element of the government's economic strategy was its programme of nationalisation. Labour platforms had long echoed to calls for 'the public ownership of the means of production and distribution', and the 1945 manifesto had outlined a specific 'shopping list' of industries it was proposed to nationalise within the lifetime of a parliament. Public ownership was justified on two grounds: in order to turn some major concerns into service industries, operated for the benefit of the whole community, rather than simply for profit; and in order to redeem certain industries – coal being the prime example – alleged to have been inefficient in private hands. These arguments had a powerful appeal at the end of the war, coming at a time when the state had already assumed much greater responsibility over the economic affairs of the nation. Hence during 1945–46 the government, under the guidance of Herbert Morrison, was able to push ahead with a major legislative programme:

NATIONALISATION MEASURES, 1945–51

Industry	2nd Reading of Bill	Vesting Day	Numbers employed
Bank of England	29 Oct. 1945	1 Mar. 1946	6,700
Coal	29 Jan. 1946	1 Jan. 1947	765,000
Civil aviation	6 May 1946	1 Aug. 1946	23,300
Cable and wireless	21 May 1945	1 Jan. 1947	9,500
Transport	16 Dec. 1946	1 Jan. 1948	888,000
Electricity	3 Feb. 1947	1 Apr. 1948	176,000
Gas	10 Feb. 1948	1 Apr. 1949	143,500
Iron and steel	15 Nov. 1948	15 Feb. 1951	292,000

Source: D. N. Chester (**46**)

Initially, nationalisation encountered little serious resistance. When Hugh Dalton proposed new terms for the Bank of England, arguing that 'the Old Man of the Treasury and the Old Lady of Threadneedle Street should be legally married', Conservatives in Parliament expressed few complaints (**43**). But it would be wrong to assume, as some historians have, that public ownership in general was uncontroversial, developing as a shared aim owing to wartime experience. Churchill's coalition had, in fact, deliberately avoided discussing the post-war ownership of industry, as it was considered too controversial. Indeed, as the Opposition gradually recovered its strength after 1945, so it put up increasingly stern resistance to nationalisation, which was depicted as distorting the performance of Britain's private-enterprise economy. By the time Labour came to take gas into public hands in 1948, much of the government's early confidence about the value of nationalisation was evaporating, and the Conservatives introduced some 800 amendments in an effort to defeat the bill. Hugh Gaitskell, in charge of piloting the legislation through the House of Commons, became so provoked by Tory tactics that he caused an uproar at one point by comparing one of his opponents to Hitler (**20, 46**).

In the meantime, much of the detail of Labour's policy, including the public-corporation form of management adopted for nationalised industries, reflected a further element in the government's economic strategy – its desire to conciliate the trade-union movement. The instinctive loyalty of many union leaders to the new government was reinforced early on when the Cabinet introduced legislation to repeal the 1927 Trade Disputes Act. This was a move of profound symbolic importance, removing the worst features of what was considered a vindictive measure of revenge by Conservative ministers after the defeat of the General Strike. Instead, the principle of 'contracting out'* from union levies to Labour funds was restored, helping to bolster party finances, and restrictions on secondary industrial action were relaxed. The new legislation was clearly central to the establishment of much closer government–union relations than had existed before the war; in return for the repeal of the Trade Disputes Act, union leaders took a lead in urging wage restraint on their members for much of the lifetime of the parliament (**54, 56**). Although improvements had occurred after 1939, when labour became indispensable to boosting production, there was no guarantee that wartime advances would continue with the ending of hostilities. On several occasions during the war Churchill had ruled out any amendment of the 1927 Act, acting under pressure from Conservative back-benchers, whose hard-line attitude towards trade-union law persisted after 1945. The mixed and 'corporate' economy, in other words, was more the product of Attlee's than of Churchill's premiership.

By the same token, Labour's welfare programme went beyond wartime orthodoxy in some, though not all, respects. During the war, Conservatives had initially been sceptical about the main thrust of the 1942 Beveridge Report – the idea of providing social security 'from the cradle to the grave', in place of the haphazard system of benefits available before the war. By 1945 Conservative spokesmen agreed – along with the other parties – that a more streamlined system must be introduced, although Churchill still hoped that the Beveridge plan might be refined in a 'non-socialist' direction (**97**). One of Labour's first priorities after returning to power was to ensure the passage into law of the 1946 National Insurance Act, piloted through the Commons by Welshman James Griffiths, who had been prominent in refining the party's policy on social insurance during the war. The new measure was based on the principle of universality, in place of pre-war selectivity, and brought together for the first time a comprehensive range of benefits to provide insurance against sickness, unemployment and old age (**94**). Griffiths presented the reform as the 'beginning of the establishment of the principle of a National Minimum Standard' – a view clearly shared by Labour back-benchers, who pressurised the minister into setting pension levels above those originally suggested by Beveridge (**93**). Although open controversy on this topic was limited, there was no doubt that the respective party spokesmen still viewed the reform from different perspectives. For Labour MPs, the later addition of 'national assistance' to the new system was essential in providing a safety net for those unable to meet the required insurance payments. But in the eyes of Conservatives, means-tested national assistance was a crucial safeguard against the threat of 'scrounging' (**47**). Labour's reform certainly brought with it fresh problems, notably that of maintaining the level of benefits in the face of rising inflation. Nevertheless, at the time of the 1950 election, Labour propaganda could make much of the claim that social security had eradicated the most abject destitution of the 1930s (**50**).

Education was a second area where Labour ministers, on the whole, were content to develop lines of policy already mapped out before 1945. Attention in the educational world centred on the implementation of the 1944 Act, an agreed coalition measure enshrining the principle that, for the first time, all children over the age of eleven should receive free secondary schooling. A small, but vocal, minority of Labour opinion believed that equality of opportunity would remain elusive unless all children attended the same type of local, 'multilateral' schools, instead of the 'tripartite system' – grammar, secondary modern and technical schools – favoured by ministers and officials. Indeed Ellen Wilkinson, and her successor as Education Minister in 1947, George Tomlinson, have subsequently been accused of delaying the introduction of comprehensive schooling for a generation (**61**). In the immediate post-war years, however, most Labour supporters still hoped that parity of esteem between different types of secondary institution might be attainable, multilateral schools were seen primarily as a worthwhile experiment. It was only later, as the new school system became operational, that mainstream party opinion came to the view that secondary moderns could not compete with the prestigious grammar schools; the resulting social divisiveness, it was agreed, could only be tackled by the wholesale introduction of comprehensive schools (**39**, **41**). In the meantime, Attlee's ministers concentrated on short-term objectives. Before her unexpected death in 1947, Ellen Wilkinson secured agreement for the raising of the school-leaving age to fifteen; and in spite of mounting concern about the costs of reform, increased Treasury funds were still made available for education, notably to update school buildings suffering from war damage and years of neglect (**51**, **104**).

Other areas of policy had a much more distinct ideological cutting edge. This slowly became apparent in the case of housing and town planning, responsibility for which rested – as it had before 1939 – with the Ministry of Health. The combination of housing and health inevitably imposed great pressures on the new minister, Aneurin Bevan, who soon came under attack for failing to tackle housing shortages; a population enlarged by a million was now crowded into 700,000 fewer properties, owing to destruction or damage during the war (**88**). Without doubt, Labour's housing programme got off to a poor start. Aside from the difficulties of obtaining raw materials, Bevan ran up against a host of political and administrative difficulties, with different ministers wishing to see scarce resources channelled first towards factories or hospitals rather than housing. After a year in office, the government had failed to meet its own target for new houses, and criticism of the minister mounted as many homeless families – frustrated by lack of progress – began a spontaneous squatting movement in various parts of the country. But by 1947 the position was beginning to improve, and Bevan's objectives became clearer. In a conscious effort to favour working-class families, attention was deliberately shifted from private house-building – the priority of the 1930s – towards the local-authority rented sector. Four out of every five houses built under the Labour government were to be council properties, constructed to more generous specifications than before the war. This, together with subsidies which kept down council rents, gave public-sector housing its biggest boost yet and further benefited lower wage earners. Labour policy also antagonised the Conservative Opposition on broader questions of planning the environment. Some sections of the town-and-country-planning legislation of 1946–47, which sought to introduce more orderly land development and establish new towns to ease population congestion, were eventually repealed after Churchill came back to power in 1951 (**53, 92**). Bevan thus came to have a defensible and distinct record in housing. Over a million new homes were built in the six years after the war, and if there was some disappointment about the speed of reform, then part of the reason for this was the priority accorded to what became the centrepiece of Labour's welfare programme – the National Health Service (NHS).

Health provision had developed haphazardly in Britain before the war. Health insurance, introduced in 1911, covered less than half the working population by 1939, and the medical cover provided was not available to the dependants – wives and children – of those who could afford to make insurance contributions. The stresses of war confirmed the need for reform, and coalition ministers agreed in principle to the idea of a comprehensive health service, free at the point of use. But the means to such an end remained contentious, and the proposals outlined by Bevan within weeks of his appointment in 1945 indicated a determination to go beyond wartime plans in some important respects (**14, 20**). Most notably, the minister aimed at a stroke to bring the fee-paying, independent 'voluntary' hospitals into one state system – a move strongly opposed by the Conservative Party. Reform of the hospitals became a central element of the 1946 National Health Service Act, which also introduced free access to general-practitioner treatment and to local-authority services, such as maternity care and child welfare. The Act was enthusiastically endorsed by Labour MPs as the realisation of a long-standing aim, though the minister was not without his critics. Conservative back-benchers voted against the bill, arguing that it 'retards the development of hospital services by destroying local ownership' (**63**). In the period before the NHS began to operate in July 1948, such complaints were taken up vociferously by members of the British Medical Association, who denounced Bevan as the 'Tito of Tonypandy'* (**32, 38**). As a result, he was forced to make certain concessions – such as allowing capitation fees rather than state salary to remain the basis of doctors' remuneration – thereby disturbing party stalwarts in the Socialist Medical Association. But Bevan's achievement remained beyond question. In the face of conflicting demands and pressures, he had demonstrated that there was nothing irreconcilable between socialism and pragmatic, popular reform [**doc. 5**].

The post-war settlement was therefore to a considerable extent Labour's achievement. Wartime developments had helped to create a new intellectual climate, one more favourable to state welfare than had existed in the 1930s, but the shape and extent of reform still owed much to Labour's tradition of democratic socialism, whatever its anomalies (**3**). Where Churchill's coalition, over the course of five years, produced primarily a series of compromise proposals, Attlee's government within the space of months actually forged a new economic and social order. This was achieved, moreover, in the face of some stern resistance. It follows that had there been a genuine wartime consensus on domestic policy, then much of Labour's programme would have been less contentious than proved the case. If Churchill had remained in power as the 'man who won the war' – as many commentators predicted – all the indicators were that the Conservatives would have opted for a far more cautious reform programme. Indeed, it has been argued that a post-war Conservative government was more likely to follow the pattern of the Lloyd George coalition after the First World War, introducing some early measures of social change but then retreating once the economy ran into problems.

> Britain after 1945 was a less tension ridden, more unified society than that which emerged after the Lloyd George era after 1918, overlain as the latter was by the aura of corruption and adventurism. This time, the vision of a 'land fit for heroes' . . . was not wantonly forgotten or betrayed (**20**).

The value of the post-war settlement has, like its origins, been much contested. Critics argue that Attlee's reform package contained some glaring weaknesses. Newly nationalised industries, for instance, were not used as a lever for controlling the whole economy, and some 80 per cent of industry still remained in private hands. The failure, moreover, to address the iniquities of the class system – leaving untouched the civil service, public schools and the monarchy – meant there had been no meaningful advance towards the stated aim of a 'socialist commonwealth' (**10**, **18**, **30**). There was no doubt that reform could have gone further in some respects, and that legislation brought unforeseen difficulties. In particular, rapidly escalating costs were soon to force ministers into adopting the unwelcome language of restraint; the result was that in 1951 Labour left behind 'several imposing chunks of masonry instead of the complete welfare edifice it had hoped to build' (**52**). The advances were nevertheless real. Within eighteen months, Attlee's Cabinet had done more than any previous twentieth-century government to improve the lot of ordinary working people. Although the principle of universal benefits meant disproportionate gains for middle-class families, for the majority of the population welfare reform after 1945 offered family allowances, free medical treatment, subsidised housing and educational opportunities on a scale not known before (**22**). Judged against the standards of the 1930s, and in view of the financial disaster that threatened at the end of the war, Labour ministers could reflect with great pride on the early months of their administration. For Hugh Dalton, 1946 was Labour's 'Annus Mirabilis' [**doc. 6**]. The Chancellor was soon to discover, however, that fortunes in politics could change rapidly. After the progress of 1946, the following year was to bring something rather different – a period of sustained crisis.

4   The Economic and Political Crises of 1947

The government's honeymoon period came to an abrupt end in 1947. For several months after the election victory of July 1945, as we have seen, Labour ministers energetically set about introducing the party's domestic programme. More than seventy Acts of Parliament reached the statute book during the 1945–46 session, and the government's buoyancy was enhanced by signs that Britain's economy was making an early recovery from the traumas of war. Exports in 1946 more than doubled over the previous year; capital investment in industry was resuming apace; and unemployment remained low in spite of the pressures of demobilisation. Indeed, alone among the major combatants in Europe, British industrial output in 1946 had already recovered to its pre-war level (**55, 57**). This did not mean that critics of the government had been entirely silenced. A world shortage of grain, for instance, led to the introduction of bread rationing in 1946: a move which resulted in the resignation of the Minister of Food and a slump in the Labour vote at the Bexley 'bread-rationing' by-election (**6**). Aspects of Dalton's economic policy were also the subject of much hostile comment, notably his insistence on low interest rates or 'cheap money' as a means of stimulating domestic revival. The Chancellor had little time for City experts who argued that cheap money was inflationary – a claim, he felt, that disguised opposition to welfare reform – though in time circumstances did force a modification of monetary policy (**101**). Mounting criticism, however, had not detracted from Dalton's exuberance at the despatch box in 1946, and few could predict the suddenness with which his fortunes were to change. For in 1947 the government, and the Chancellor in particular, were to find themselves much more on the defensive. The sense of crisis was such that 1947 marked an important transition: from the confident progress of the early months to a new, less buoyant, phase in the history of the Attlee administration.

The government's troubles in 1947 arose from a combination of external factors, over which individuals had little or no control, and incompetence on the part of senior ministers. Nowhere was this more evident than in the case of the so-called 'winter crisis'. From early in 1946, government officials had been concerned about Britain's increasingly inadequate coal supplies; unless remedied, it was believed this problem might provoke a fuel shortage, with disastrous consequences for industry (**45, 96**). The seriousness of the situation was just becoming public knowledge when, at the beginning of 1947, Britain was confronted by its severest spell of cold weather for over fifty years. From late January through to mid-March, much of the country remained in the grip of frequent and abnormally heavy snowfalls, biting frosts and bitterly cold winds. With the River Thames frozen over, innumerable villages cut off and tra el made hazardous, the government soon had to resort to emergency measures. In February it was announced that because of coal shortages and the difficulties of transportation, electricity was to be limited to certain hours of the day for domestic consumers and cut off altogether to industry in some regions. This situation was to persist for several weeks before the weather finally relented; by that time, however, the damage to the government's reputation had already been done:

> As industrial activity declined and unemployment rose, and as the standards of household comfort and public amenity declined; as milk and mail deliveries became uncertain; as people actually passed out in the streets from the effects of the biting cold; . . . as even Big Ben refused to mark the passage of time in due form because his works were iced up; as adversity piled upon hardship in a seemingly endless catalogue of misfortune, people began to look for somebody to blame (**58**).

It was not long before the finger was being pointed at one man in particular – the Minister of Fuel and Power, Emanuel Shinwell – though none of Labour's ministers emerged with much credit from the whole episode. Attlee had in fact been receiving warnings from his advisers about the developing fuel crisis for several months past, but accepted until late in the day reassurances from Shinwell that coal stocks would pick up (**95, 96**). The Minister of Fuel and Power, it must be said, had few easy options in 1946. The only certain method of avoiding shortages was to impose immediate restrictions; the inevitable rise in unemployment that would result was ruled out as politically unacceptable in a year of great export recovery (**103**). But criticism of Shinwell remained well-founded. Apart from complacency until matters had become irretrievable, he clearly overlooked the demand side of the coal issue, placing his faith instead in massive productivity gains that never materialised. Although he later tried to blame others, both party colleagues and the Opposition were in no doubt that the minister bore primary responsibility for the scale of the fuel crisis [**doc. 7**]. Conservative propagandists, eager to seize this first major opportunity since Labour came to power, coined the popular slogan 'Shiver with Shinwell'. One Conservative peer, speaking in the House of Lords, struck a particular chord when he described the cause of the crisis as 'not an act of God, but the inactivity of Emanuel' (**24**).

Shinwell's reputation never recovered from such attacks, and he was to be removed from his post before the year was out. The winter crisis also had much wider repercussions. Later estimates put the total loss of industrial output in the first three months of 1947 at some 25 per cent − a severe blow to a government bent on stimulating growth. This, in turn, cost the nation 200 million pounds in lost exports, thereby contributing to a balance-of-payments problem that was certain to be magnified with the advent of convertibility later in the year. In the short term, the government also suffered from a natural degree of public disenchantment. A typical attitude recorded by the social survey group, Mass-Observation, in the midst of the crisis was that of a young ex-serviceman. 'I wish I were anywhere but in this goddamned country', he lamented, 'where there is nothing but queues and restrictions and forms and shortages and no food and cold' (**58**). Many voters, however, were more inclined to blame the weather rather than ministers for their misfortunes, and a modest fall in the government's opinion-poll rating was soon to be recovered. Perhaps more significant, politically, was the toll which events had taken on the confidence of Labour ministers and supporters. After carrying all before them in 1946, ministers were suddenly confronted, if only temporarily, by economic ills that socialist planning seemed entirely powerless to remedy; it was no coincidence that the 'Keep Left' group of MPs now urged the need for more drastic policies upon the government (**29**, **31**). 'This had not been the end of the world, as some panic-mongers had expected,' reflected the Chancellor. 'But it was certainly the first really heavy blow to confidence in the Government and in our post-war plans .... Never glad, confident morning again!' (**90**).

The spring, and the return to more normal weather conditions, brought fresh difficulties. In the absence of Herbert Morrison, out of action for several weeks with a serious illness, unrest on the backbenches began to intensify, especially over foreign policy. And Cabinet discussions about the public ownership of iron and steel in

April 1947 revealed some deep divisions over future strategy. As a late inclusion in the 1945 manifesto, iron and steel was by far the most controversial area of Labour's nationalisation programme. Resistance to the government was led by a powerful group of steel masters, determined to protect the profitability of their large-scale, monopolistic industry, and backed up by vociferous Conservative opposition in Parliament. In 1946 the Minister of Supply, John Wilmot, announced the establishment of an Iron and Steel Control Board to oversee the industry, pending any firm announcement about public ownership (**43**, **46**). This step-by-step approach reflected Cabinet differences: some, like Morrison, were concerned that impressive rises in steel production might be jeopardised by imposing new controls; others such as the Chancellor favoured swift and decisive action. A socialist economy, Dalton argued, was only feasible if the government lifted its sights beyond the public utilities. 'Practical socialism in Britain', he said, 'only really began with coal and with iron and steel, two cases where there was a specially strong argument for breaking the power of a most reactionary body of capitalists' (**90**). Under strong pressure from the parliamentary party, many of whom regarded this as a litmus test of socialist commitment, the Cabinet finally announced in August 1947 that nationalisation would go ahead, scheduled to take place in the 1948–49 parliamentary session at the earliest (**29**). By this stage, there were already signs that ministerial opinion was hardening against further, wholesale extensions of the public sector; the idea of 'consolidating' existing gains was beginning to take hold (**20**). In the autumn of 1947, however, government attention was focused not on long-term policy but on one immediate, and potentially disastrous, question – the so-called 'convertibility crisis'.

Dalton's handling of the economy came under growing pressure after the fuel crisis, especially as he appeared powerless to prevent a rapidly deteriorating balance-of-payments position. This stemmed primarily from a trade imbalance which left the United States as the major supplier of food and raw materials after the war. As North American imports flooded in, British exports failed to keep pace, with the result that more than half of the American loan was swept away in the first half of 1947; the remainder now looked as if it would run out in a matter of months. Superimposed on this problem was the even graver threat caused by convertibility, which came into effect in July, one year after the ratification of the loan by Congress. Coming at a moment when Britain's gold and dollar reserves were dwindling rapidly, the free convertibility of pounds into dollars caused havoc (**45**). Within days sterling was under intense pressure, and as a huge outflow of capital began there was talk of 'another 1931'. The Chancellor's reassurances that modest import cuts would salvage the situation cut little ice, and during August 1947 the drain of dollars became so rapid that the British economy faced ruination. By the end of the month, Dalton was forced to retreat. The suspension of convertibility was announced, and the government declared its intention to eliminate many North American commodities from the British market, thereby imposing further restrictions on the hard-pressed consumer. The Chancellor recognised that the suspension of convertibility was a humiliation from which his reputation was unlikely to recover, especially as he was forced to follow it up with an emergency budget which heralded a new era of spending controls and counter-inflationary devices (**42, 48**). 'No Chancellor in history', gloated one of his opponents, 'has seen a more disastrous end to his financial policy than Mr Dalton' (**101**).

The Chancellor, and his 'irresponsible' domestic programme, thus carried the can for the second economic crisis of 1947, just as the Minister of Fuel and Power had for the coal shortage earlier in the year (**49**). The parallels should not, though, be overdrawn. Dalton, on the advice of his Treasury officials, certainly underestimated the effects of convertibility, but – unlike Shinwell – he had spent many months warning Cabinet colleagues about the dangers ahead. 'We are', he noted early in 1947, 'drifting in a state of semi-animation towards the rapids. We have started our course, since the last election, wonderfully well. But we look like finishing wonderfully badly – worse, perhaps, than in 1931' (**102**). Dalton consistently made the case in Cabinet that domestic reform, though slowed down, must be protected as the *raison d'être* of the government; major reductions should be made instead in military spending, still running at high levels in the aftermath of war. But cutbacks in overseas expenditure were strongly resisted by Bevin, the Foreign Secretary, often supported by Attlee, who himself came under pressure for failing to give a strong lead as the crisis developed. Other ministers were also culpable. Herbert Morrison later reinforced the idea that Treasury mismanagement was at the heart of the problem [**doc. 8**]. As Lord President, however, with responsibility for co-ordinating economic policy, Morrison was still struggling with the administrative machinery for planning in the summer of 1947, and his biographers conclude that to an extent 'Morrison himself must take the main blame' (**44, 91**). In retrospect, there was much substance in the argument – used by Dalton at the time – that Britain was ultimately the victim of terms reluctantly accepted as part of the US loan, and that 1947 was a much better moment than 1945 to face up to unavoidable realities. But in the search for scapegoats, it was inevitable that the Chancellor, and to a lesser extent Morrison, should shoulder responsibility, and find their places in the senior Cabinet hierarchy under threat. This became clearer when the public drama of convertibility was followed, behind the scenes, by an unexpected political crisis: nothing less than an attempt to remove the Prime Minister.

The principal mover in the attempted 'palace revolution' against Attlee was Sir Stafford Cripps, the only senior minister whose reputation grew steadily during 1947. Cripps, already considered dynamic at the Board of Trade, made a particularly strong impression by exhorting the nation to new endeavours as the economic crisis developed over the summer. He was now seen, in short, 'as he had always seen himself: as a saviour' (**96**, **101**). Cripps had gradually come to the conclusion that the government lacked strong direction in its co-ordination of economic planning. Initially this meant dissatisfaction with the responsible minister, Morrison, but as events unfolded Cripps decided that only stronger leadership than the Prime Minister seemed to offer would suffice. In early September, he approached two senior colleagues, Dalton and Morrison, to ask if they would support a plan to replace Attlee with Ernest Bevin, whose experience gave him unique experience of domestic and foreign policy. The Chancellor was tempted by this proposal, and indeed floated the idea to Bevin himself, only to be met with a blunt display of loyalty to the party leader. 'Who do you think I am?' Bevin retorted, 'Lloyd George?' At this point, backing for the putative Cripps plan began to crumble. Dalton would go no further unless Morrison pledged support, but the Lord President, who continued to have leadership ambitions of his own, would have nothing to do with a scheme aimed at elevating his long-standing antagonist, the Foreign Secretary (**20**, **96**).

In spite of such discouragement, Cripps decided to go ahead alone. On the evening of 9 September, he boldly confronted Attlee with the suggestion that Bevin should take over as Prime Minister in order to invigorate government policy on the home front. Attlee, in a masterfully cool response, picked up the telephone to enquire whether Bevin had any desire to succeed as leader. After receiving confirmation that Bevin entertained no such wish, the Prime Minister – without any hint of embarrassment – conceded that a fresh approach was required in order to galvanise the economy. Herbert, he believed, was not really up to the task; would Stafford therefore accept the post of economic overlord? Cripps was no doubt taken aback by this sudden turning of the tables, but with his 'egotism of the altruist', he had little hesitation in accepting. Within the government, Hugh Dalton noted in his diary, 'the movement, begun by Cripps with my support, to put Bevin in Attlee's place, has now turned into a movement to put Cripps in Morrison's place' (**102**). The Prime Minister once more reigned without challenge, though he must have become conscious of his increasing political dependence on the loyalty of the Foreign Secretary. Cripps had entered Downing Street a rebel, and emerged only minutes later as Attlee's right-hand man (**95**).

This high political drama reflected the strains imposed on relationships between the 'big five' by events during 1947. Attlee's swift action on 9 September, though often regarded as spontaneous, was almost certainly thought out in advance. For several weeks over the summer the parliamentary lobbies and newspapers were buzzing with rumours about challenges to the Prime Minister. Attlee therefore had time to prepare his defences, and to decide that Morrison must be relieved of some of his responsibilities. Although not presented in terms of a demotion, the rise of Cripps – who now became Minister of Economic Affairs – naturally provoked speculation that Morrison had been snubbed (**91**). Nor did the Prime Minister forget that his Chancellor had been an accessory to conspiracy. Dalton, overburdened by the convertibility episode and contemplating resignation, had flirted with a scheme that might allow him to escape the Treasury, perhaps taking over from Bevin at the Foreign Office. He was no longer a bullish, confident figure, and prior to introducing his emergency budget of November 1947 he made a fatal blunder. Shortly before delivering his speech in the Commons, the Chancellor revealed details of the budget to a lobby correspondent. When this breach of parliamentary convention was revealed, the Conservative Opposition decided to launch a strong campaign of protest, and within days Dalton had resigned, to be replaced at the Treasury by Cripps. Attlee later claimed that he accepted the resignation as a matter of principle, though other ministers had survived far graver offences. The Chancellor's willingness to countenance an alternative leader, together with the failings of his economic stewardship, clearly made him vulnerable. 'The Prime Minister accepted Dalton's resignation', concludes Ben Pimlott, 'because he wanted to be rid of him' (**101**).

Resignation from high office marked the culmination of a terrible

31

year for Dalton. If 1946 had been Labour's 'Annus Mirabilis', then 1947, he later commented, was 'Annus Horrendus' [**doc. 9**]. The year had not been entirely devoid of legislative achievement. Nationalisation of the transport and electricity industries; a major new initiative in agricultural policy; and the Town and Country Planning Act, which gave rise to the introduction of new towns as a means of relieving urban overcrowding – all these measures indicated an administration with a continuing sense of purpose and direction. But there was no doubt that the momentum of the Attlee government had been disrupted. In the months between the fuel crisis and Dalton's resignation, ministers were faced with an increasingly hostile press and a gradual erosion of public confidence. In August 1947 the Conservatives overtook Labour in national opinion polls for the first time since Attlee came to power, and by-election results reflected a pronounced swing towards the Tories (**6**). Local elections in November confirmed the trend. With Labour losing nearly 700 seats, Churchill was able to present the results as a 'nation-wide protest against Socialist mismanagement' (**95**).

Changes in public opinion were to help in reinforcing a perceptible shift in government style. After the buoyant expansionism of 1945–46, the remainder of the government's term in office was to be marked by more cautious advance; the legacy of 1947 was 'the age of austerity'. This division between the first and second halves of the Attlee administration was also sharpened by a changing balance of power in the Cabinet. The left found itself weakened by Attlee's reshuffle following the 'September plot': Shinwell was replaced at Fuel and Power by his more moderate junior minister, Hugh Gaitskell, widely seen as a rising star in the party. And by the end of the year Hugh Dalton, 'the most left-wing member of the big five', according to one leading Whitehall insider, had also gone, and had been replaced by a Chancellor who had fewer qualms about the need for tightening the belt (**21, 101**). The Prime Minister and his new team of senior ministers were thus compelled towards 'consolidation' by the pressure of events in 1947. Attlee had survived unscathed at the helm, and his leadership was henceforth to be secure. But he was never quite the same force again. Certainly, in fending off his critics, the Prime Minister had become ever more reliant upon the one colleague whose authority matched his own, the man who had been playing a critical role in reshaping the post-war international order – Ernest Bevin.

5 Ernest Bevin and Overseas Policy

The Second World War had profoundly altered the balance of world power. With Germany occupied and dismembered in the wake of Hitler's defeat, the global influence of Europe had been diminished at the expense of the victorious superpowers, the United States and the Soviet Union. Britain too, as Churchill well realised before he left office, had paid an enormous price in helping to defeat Nazism. Events since 1939, as we have seen, had exhausted Britain's economic resources, and the indispensable role played by the Americans and Russians – culminating in the use of the first atomic weapons* against Japan – served to underline the military superiority of the superpowers by 1945. In overseas policy, therefore, Britain would clearly have to face up to some major adjustments; it was no longer possible, as in the past, to adopt a mediating role aimed at preserving the balance of power in Europe. But to set against this, the outcome of the war still left Britain with the perception of itself as a great power. British troops had, after all, been on hand to receive the surrender of large numbers of German, Italian and Japanese forces, and the survival of the Empire emphasised the point that British interests stretched to all corners of the world. With the Prime Minister sitting alongside the Americans and Russians as the peacemaking process got under way, Britain could still regard itself as being among the 'big three', even if no longer in the 'top two'. In these circumstances, it was natural that Attlee's government should expect to play a leading role in tackling some of the complex and urgent problems of post-war policy: the need for a lasting settlement that would fill the power vacuum in Central Europe, the question of how to restore devastated economies, and the difficulty of constructing a new system of international security designed to prevent global conflict in future (**65**).

This was the scale of the task facing Ernest Bevin, who was unexpectedly chosen by Attlee to become Foreign Secretary after Labour's election victory. Bevin, whose experience had been primarily in domestic politics, was originally earmarked for the Treasury, but at the last moment he was chosen for the Foreign

Office in preference to Hugh Dalton. This was partly due to Attlee's willingness to listen to the views of the King, who objected to Dalton, though the Prime Minister later claimed that at a time when Britain faced such grave problems on the world stage, he also required a character of immense force as Foreign Secretary (**101**, **106**). Bevin certainly lived up to this requirement. He brought with him into office an unrivalled forcefulness and determination to succeed, not to mention an enormous capacity for hard work that belied his constantly poor health. His doctor described him as suffering from 'cardiac failure, arterio-sclerosis, sinusitis, enlarged liver, damaged kidneys and high blood pressure. He was overweight, smoked and drank more than was good for him, took no exercise and was a poor sleeper.' Some critics have alleged that Bevin was intellectually ill-equipped for the Foreign Office, and that his strong prejudices could easily be moulded to the wishes of senior officials (**30**). But this much underestimates his strength of personality. In practice, Bevin was to be responsible for the broad outline of all major policy initiatives after 1945, with the exception of India; indeed his constant references to 'my foreign policy' reflected his ability to impose himself on Cabinet colleagues as well as on civil servants (**79**).

Bevin's close relationship with Attlee was of particular importance in the shaping of foreign policy. During and after 1947, the Prime Minister was consistently to be found supporting Bevin against demands for reductions in defence spending; a reflection at least in part of Attlee's dependence upon the Foreign Secretary in the face of challenges to his leadership (**101**). But it should be wrong to underestimate the extent to which the two men concurred on the main lines of policy. These were essentially twofold. In the first place, once it became clear that the Anglo-American-Soviet wartime alliance was breaking down, there was a growing conviction that Britain's post-war security and economic recovery depended on the maintenance of good relations with Washington. And secondly, it was agreed that Britain's imperial commitments must be scaled down, though precisely how and where was still unclear in 1945. Opinions about the outcome have been sharply divided (**69**). For some, Bevin was to be amongst the front rank of British Foreign Secretaries; it was due to him that, for one last short period, Britain was able to play a truly influential role on the world stage (**21**, **84**). But others have found Bevin's strident nationalism and anti-communist rhetoric less appealing, claiming that he was responsible for fomenting the divisions of the Cold War. He was, moreover, only superficially committed to colonial self-government, with the result that Labour's imperial policy was at best a cynical attempt to maintain national interests through a series of unavoidable concessions (**30, 73**). In looking at the unfolding of policy in order to assess these conflicting interpretations, the year 1947 emerges – as in domestic politics – as an important dividing point.

For many months after arriving at the Foreign Office, Bevin encountered serious difficulties in his relations with both the superpowers. In spite of a reputation, deriving from his days as a trade-union boss, for strong anti-communism, Bevin hoped at the outset that Britain could continue its wartime alliance with the Soviet Union. But any prospect of 'left speaking to left' rapidly disappeared. British distrust developed gradually during 1946 as it became clear that Stalin, far from withdrawing his forces from Germany and Eastern Europe, intended to establish a series of satellite, one-party states. Soviet leaders, for their part, were suspicious of Britain's 'imperialistic' designs – for example, in the Balkans and the Middle East, where large numbers of troops were still stationed. Matters were not helped by the cool personal relationship between the Foreign Secretary and his Soviet counterpart, Molotov, whom Bevin was to describe as a 'crook'. Above all, it was the issue of defeated Germany which exacerbated the breakdown of diplomatic goodwill. The Labour government, while having little instinctive sympathy for Germany at the end of the war, recognised the importance of stimulating economic recovery in the devastated regions of Central Europe. As a result, Bevin began to press for the zones of control established in Germany to become linked economically; when the Soviet Union refused to participate in such a process, the scene was set for the creation of two separate German states. Efforts to breath new life into the Anglo-Soviet wartime alliance thus came to nothing. Instead, the existence of an 'iron curtain' – a phrase first used by Churchill – was inexorably dividing West and East, and by 1947 Bevin had concluded that the greatest danger to European stability was no longer Germany but an expansionist Soviet Union (**75, 82**).

It would be wrong to assume, however, that Britain's relations with its other major wartime ally, the United States, ran smoothly from the outset. There was a long-standing suspicion amongst Labour activists of the USA as the centre of international finance capital; this was more than reciprocated in the summer of 1945 by American fears of 'socialism' in Britain. The abrupt termination of Lend-Lease* aroused fears that President Truman's administration was about to retreat into isolationism, as had occurred with such disastrous consequences after the First World War (**20**). Bevin therefore had to expend considerable energy in attempting to persuade the Americans to maintain their commitment in occupied Europe. For the time being, suspicions remained on both sides. The United States drove a hard bargain in granting the Attlee government its crucial post-war loan, while Bevin's doubts about American reliability were fuelled by the refusal of first Truman and then Congress to collaborate on the development of nuclear weapons. This refusal, together with the assumption that, as a great power, Britain must remain abreast of the latest weapons technology, helps to explain the British decision to develop an independent nuclear capacity; a commitment made in secret by senior ministers, and not to become the subject of public discussion and dissension for several years (**68**, **72**). It was not until early 1947 that Soviet intransigence – especially over the future of Germany – made the American administration more amenable to Bevin's urgings of unity (**64**, **82**, **84**).

The difficulties confronting the Foreign Secretary in his relations with the superpowers were reflected in unease on the Labour backbenches. Indeed, foreign policy was a source of much greater controversy for the PLP at this stage than the domestic programme rapidly proceeding through Parliament. The steady erosion of confidence between West and East was particularly unwelcome to those who were advocates of a 'socialist foreign policy'; the belief promulgated in 1945 that a Labour government could exercise its influence on the world stage to help undermine the aggressive, capitalist forces that allegedly produced war. This view was held most strongly by a small number of Marxist sympathisers, but it was also shared by a larger group of about fifty MPs who formed the nucleus of what became the Keep Left movement (**29**, **31**). In November 1946, members of this group, such as Richard Crossman, Michael Foot and Ian Mikardo, decided to table an amendment in the Commons calling for a recasting of foreign policy in order to provide 'a democratic and constructive socialist alternative to an otherwise inevitable conflict between American capitalism and Soviet communism'. In essence, these critics were advocates of a European 'third force', intended to be independent of both the Americans and Russians. Bevin, out of the country at the time, responded in typically bruising fashion by calling the amendment a 'stab in the back' [**doc. 10**]; a reply which tended to obscure his support for European economic recovery. In the event, the amendment was not forced to a division, but it came against a background of concern about several aspects of government policy – not least its handling of imperial relations.

During the Second World War, the Labour Party had replaced its traditional anti-imperialism with a programme for long-term colonial development. But any aspirations towards progressive self-government were severely put to the test in the Middle East. In the case of Palestine particularly, where the British 'Mandate'* remained in operation, Bevin inherited an intractable problem; and also a further obstacle to improved relations with the Americans. Traditional tensions between the Arab majority and Jewish settlers in Palestine were suddenly escalated as Jews fled *en masse* from the horrors of Nazi Europe. Labour Party opinion was broadly in favour of the creation of a Jewish state within Palestine; and pressure from the United States, with its strong Zionist lobby, worked in the same direction. Hence President Truman urged Bevin to act upon the report of a specially appointed Anglo-American Palestine Committee, which suggested in May 1946 that immigration certificates be granted to up to 100,000 Jews. But the Foreign Secretary's response was cool. Cabinet members readily accepted the view of the Foreign Office that the importance of the Middle East to Britain, both strategically and economically, made the continuance of good relations with Arab states in the region paramount (**76**).

British policy therefore proved to be a grave disappointment to Zionist sympathisers. Bevin refused to step up Jewish entry into Palestine significantly, and antagonised opponents by some unnecessarily insensitive actions – such as the turning back of the ship *Exodus* with over 4,000 Jews on board – which left him open to charges of anti-Semitism. The government soon faced an *impasse*. Jewish groups were demanding unlimited immigration; many Arab leaders wanted to bar all entry; and neither side would accept compromise proposals involving some form of partition. To make matters worse, atrocities by Jewish militants – notably the bombing of the King David Hotel in Jerusalem in August 1946, resulting in ninety-one deaths – served to provoke a costly and futile campaign of British armed retaliation. As the British economy came under great strain in 1947, the Cabinet agreed that armed forces could not be kept indefinitely in Palestine; it was concluded that there was no realistic option other than to face up to the humiliation of early withdrawal. In spite of the absence of any constitutional settlement, the last British forces had left by mid-1948. Much to the embarrassment of party activists, Britain now stood accused of abandoning Palestine to communal warfare; many thousands were to die before the eventual establishment of the state of Israel in 1949 (**66**).

Although it was difficult to see any workable solution in Palestine, the manner of Britain's departure inevitably reflected badly on the government. Failure in the Middle East was offset, however, by Labour's fulfilment of its traditional commitment to self-government for India, hitherto the jewel in Britain's imperial crown. Churchill's coalition had already moved towards independence as the price of Indian support during the Second World War, and after the electoral success of Attlee – who had always taken a close personal interest in this question – it only remained a matter of when and how independence would be achieved (**85**, **95**). Initially, the Cabinet hoped to create an all-India constituent assembly that would bring together the two main bodies of political opinion, the Congress Party and the Muslim League. But, as in Palestine, communal tensions ran deep. During August 1946, protests by the Muslim League against a national assembly, which they felt would subject then to the rule of the Hindu majority, turned to violence, resulting in some 5,000 deaths (**77**). The government now feared that civil war might break out, for which the British would clearly be held responsible. After some feverish discussions, it was decided that good faith could only be maintained by announcing a definite date for British withdrawal in 1948, and by recognising the impossibility of creating a single national assembly [**doc. 11**].

In order to maintain the initiative, Attlee also decided to dismiss the Viceroy, Wavell, who was considered to be out of touch with Indian opinion. He was replaced by Lord Mountbatten, who was given sweeping powers to negotiate a new settlement. Mountbatten quickly concluded that, with events drifting towards civil disorder, plans for British withdrawal must be speeded up, and proposals for partition discussed as a matter of urgency. The Prime Minister, co-ordinating the government's response, immediately realised that the dangers of an early 'scuttle' were outweighed by the need to avoid a major conflagration (**95**). After a presence of some 300 years, the British Raj therefore came to an end in August 1947. Less than six months after the last Viceroy had entered into negotiations, the two separate states of India and Pakistan were created, both full members of the Commonwealth (**71**). This latter agreement was a crucial part of the settlement for the British. It allowed the government to present change in terms of beneficial evolution. And more important, by leaving before goodwill had been exhausted, Britain was able to maintain strong economic and military ties, thereby avoiding the protracted agony that was to characterise the imperial retreat of other European powers such as France. In the Indian sub-continent itself, independence was to be followed by considerable communal violence. But for the British, it was 'decolonisation without trauma' (**22**).

In retrospect, India was also a watershed in Labour's fortunes overseas. Until the middle of 1947, the Foreign Secretary could point to few tangible results from his endeavours. But over·the next two years, his policy increasingly assumed a more coherent form, and was to result in a series of diplomatic triumphs (**84**). At the heart of this lay steadily improving relations with the United States. The case of Germany, as we have seen, was particularly important in this context, though Anglo-American ties were also developing elsewhere in Europe. Britain's decision to evacuate troops from Greece and Turkey, for example, was accompanied by an American commitment — enshrined in the Truman Doctrine* — to assume the responsibilities bequeathed by Britain in the region. The most significant advance in 1947, however, centred on economic development in Europe. American businessmen and officials had for some time been alarmed by the weakness of the European economies in the aftermath of war, and in June the new Secretary of State, General Marshall, outlined his intention to launch a substantial aid programme. The Marshall Plan*, as Roy Douglas notes, 'was not really Marshall's plan at all, but an invitation to others to devise their own plans' (**70**). It was largely due to Bevin, who took this offer 'more seriously than did Marshall himself' (**21**), that a completely new structure for European economic recovery soon developed. After the Soviet Union had declined to become involved, the British Foreign Secretary led moves which resulted in the creation of the Organisation for European Economic Co-operation (OEEC). This not only provided an infrastructure for long-term planning, but also ensured massive injections of American capital in the short run. Altogether 12 billion dollars came to Europe by 1951; a significant proportion helping to stabilise the British economy after the financial crisis of 1947 (**24**, **74**, **81**).

In the period after his success in developing the Marshall Plan, Bevin concentrated on extending the American commitment in Europe from the economic to the military sphere. As a sign of intent, Britain helped to shape early in 1948 the Brussels Pact — a security agreement among the Western European nations designed to counter the Soviet threat. Without American backing, this new arrangement clearly lacked credibility as a deterrent, and for this reason Bevin pushed the Americans to contribute to a much stronger variation, a North Atlantic defence treaty. His efforts were greatly facilitated by the increasingly bitter atmosphere of the Cold War. Above all, the Berlin blockade, when the Soviet Union cut off access by land to the western sectors of Berlin for over a year, persuaded Congress that it was now imperative to abandon traditional isolationism. In April 1949, the United States therefore agreed to ally itself with the Brussels Treaty signatories, now joined by Canada, Iceland and Italy, in creating the North Atlantic Treaty Organisation (NATO). Although this did not impair the ability of Congress to make unilateral policy decisions, it nevertheless ensured a more formal commitment to the defence of Western Europe. The establishment of NATO, which marked the culmination of Bevin's diplomatic efforts since 1947, was broadly welcomed by British political opinion, though a small section of Labour MPs stood out against Britain's implied subservience to the United States (**69**, **84**).

A minority of Labour Party opinion – both at Westminster and in the constituencies – thus remained implacably opposed to the ·government's policy. But the complaints of the left, which have been echoed by some historians, had little impact at the time. As Labour's term of office drew to a close, activists on the centre and right of the party were inclined to share the Prime Minister's view that Bevin had been a formidable and successful Foreign Secretary [**doc. 12**]. In relation to the superpowers, as we have seen, it was not Bevin who betrayed hopes of 'left speaking to left'. Only under the pressure of events did he come to the conclusion that an Atlantic alliance was imperative, and the Americans were alarmed to find that he was still seeking ways of improving relations with the East in 1949 (**65**). Many of the Keep Left* critics were also persuaded by Soviet behaviour, notably during the Berlin blockade, that Bevin had no alternative other than to adopt a hard-line attitude (**20**, **31**). If this meant playing down the prospect of closer European integration, then this had to be set against the cementing of a 'special relationship' with the United States; an alliance that produced immediate advantages, both strategically and in economic terms. And to those in the party who were unhappy about the belligerence of his anti-communism, Bevin had some blunt answers. He did not feel obliged to take lessons in democratic socialist behaviour from those who held up Stalin as a model, and he also reminded critics that faint-heartedness was associated with appeasement – for which the left had bitterly attacked the pre-war Conservative Party. For Bevin, the outcome spoke for itself: Britain in 1950 had achieved international security of a sort that was inconceivable between the wars.

As far as the Empire was concerned, Labour's record was more mixed. The débâcle in Palestine was indicative of wider failings in the Middle East, a region which Bevin considered vital to British interests. His willingness to maintain an expensive military presence east of Suez was sceptically received, and in spite of efforts to stay on good terms with the Arab world, relations with the likes of Egypt and Iraq were increasingly tense (**76**). Nor would it be accurate to claim that Labour's actions had been motivated primarily by an altruistic desire to promote colonial self-government. Ministers were always conscious of the likely effects upon British interests, both strategic and economic, and this helps to explain why self-government was pushed forward at a much faster rate in some regions than in others. There was also, as the case of India demonstrated, a good deal of muddle in government thinking, which suggested that decolonisation was to consist more of an unplanned series of breakdowns rather than an orderly retreat (**67**). 'If, as Seely claimed, the British Empire was acquired "in a fit of absence of mind", it was lost, to judge from India's case, in a similar state of perplexity' (**80**). The practical effect of Labour policy, however, was nevertheless striking. The number of people under direct British sovereignty fell from 457 million in 1945 to only 70 million six years later, and the Colonial Office could point to its promotion of constitutional development in areas as far apart as West Africa and South-east Asia. Above all, the independence of India helped to establish the notion of a new multiracial Commonwealth, based upon more equal and flexible relationships than in the past (**20**). In imperial policy, as in relations with the superpowers, the Labour government could point to some solid achievements towards the end of its term; this at a time when problems on the home front were intensifying.

6 On the Retreat, 1948–50

Pragmatism became the chief hallmark of Labour's domestic policy after 1947. Attlee's administration in its early days had gone where previous governments feared to tread, introducing the main features of Britain's welfare state and mixed economy. But the desperately hard winter of 1947, followed by the convertibility crisis, had shaken ministerial confidence, and marked the transition to a new, more cautious phase. It would be wrong to exaggerate the extent to which policies and priorities were redefined after 1947. Expenditure on Britain's social services continued to run at historically unprecedented levels, and the government's underlying ideological purpose was still evident; for example, in the introduction of legal assistance for the poor in 1949. But the change in style and strategy could not be mistaken. The period between 1948 and the general election in 1950 became indelibly associated in the public mind with restrictions and hardships, a time when ministers used the language of restraint and 'consolidation'. Historians, following the pattern of opinion at the time, have been divided in their judgements about this 'age of austerity'. For some, a period of stability was essential in both the party and national interests, providing a solid basis upon which Labour could launch its campaign for re-election in 1950 (**20**, **21**). Critics, however, allege that ministers now moved further than ever away from the radical rhetoric of 1945, thus confirming a betrayal of socialist idealism (**10**, **18**). Here, it will be suggested that Labour's retreat after 1947 – which more so than the war years marked the origins of consensus politics – stemmed from an almost irresistible combination of forces. External, economic constraints were now coupled with the domestic considerations of seeking re-election and defeating a revitalised Conservative Party. But if consolidation was necessary, then so was renewal: the creation of a fresh vision of Labour politics for the 1950s. It was in this latter respect that the government stands most open to criticism.

The age of austerity was dominated on the home front by a single individual, Sir Stafford Cripps. His pre-eminence reflected, above all, a triumph of personality over an administration otherwise running out of steam. Until his own health gave way under the strain in 1950, Cripps set a remarkable example of conscientiousness that few could match. His prodigious work rate included three hours at the desk as Chancellor before breakfast. On one occasion, a schoolboy called saying he had an appointment at five o'clock in the morning; the policeman on the door, assuming the boy to be unbalanced, played for time. But when the visitor insisted: 'Sir Stafford Cripps asked me to come at this hour', the policeman replied: 'Oh, him. Yes, please come in' (**96**). Allied to this was a deep religious commitment; not since the days of Gladstone had any senior minister left such a strong impression that his decisions were 'imparted to him by some higher wisdom' (**96**). On a personal level, therefore, Cripps had little in common with his predecessor, epitomising as he seemed to the ideals of sacrifice and discipline that he hoped the nation would share. In policy terms, Cripps brought with him to the Treasury the approach, not of the 1930s doctrinaire socialist, but of the technocrat. His experience in high office since 1942 had led him to redefine his socialism in terms of industrial efficiency – only if productivity and exports were substantially raised, he now believed, could rising living standards be maintained and Britain made a progressively fairer society. The contrast between the 'inflationist' Dalton and the 'deflationist' Cripps can easily be overdrawn, but there was no doubt that economic and industrial policy was reshaped after 1947; a retreat to consensus was soon under way.

At the heart of the new Chancellor's strategy, deriving from his experience at the Board of Trade, was an emphasis on export growth as the key to economic success. This helps to explain his attitude towards government controls, which remained extensive in the aftermath of war. These ranged from price controls, notably over food, to labour controls and controls over production and consumption, including rationing. In spite of the relief offered by Marshall Aid, Cripps believed that the circumstances he inherited left him with no choice but to continue controlling the consumption of basic foodstuffs. He sought to present this in the collectivist, wartime rhetoric of 'fair shares', but after 1947 food rationing increasingly became a central theme of anti-government propaganda. 'Sir Austere Cripps', as his opponents called him, was held responsible for constantly lengthening queues to obtain food of dubious quality. The most notorious example came with the appearance of 'snoek', an oily and tasteless fish purchased in bulk by the government. The public refused to eat it, and though it was claimed that the whole consignment had been sold off, rumours persisted that much had been reprocessed as cat food (**7**, **32**). The Chancellor clearly believed that exhortations on the grounds of patriotic necessity – regarding the ration book as 'a badge of good citizenship' – would produce a disciplined consumer response (**22**). But he was not – as his critics alleged – a doctrinaire advocate of controls for their own sake. Cabinet ministers, including Cripps, recognised that controls were increasingly unpopular, not only with consumers but also with employers and trade unions, who regarded them as an unnecessary hindrance to the recovery of export markets. Hence in November 1948 the youthful Harold Wilson, who had succeeded Cripps as President of the Board of Trade, announced a 'bonfire of controls', removing various production controls. In 1949 this was followed up by ending the rationing of clothes and textiles (**48**, **59**).

The government's line on controls was itself part of a broader abandonment of 'economic planning'. In 1945 Labour's manifesto, *Let Us Face the Future*, had made much of the need to plan all industrial resources in the national interest. Nationalisation was seen as one essential ingredient in this context, though Dalton had taken few further planning initiatives. After 1947 Cripps, characteristically, brought much greater clarity to the government's administrative machinery for economic policy. Unlike Morrison as Lord President, he quickly resolved problems of overlapping authority and created an efficient system at Cabinet level and amongst senior civil servants (**96**). But in spite of references to this streamlined system being responsible for 'national planning', there was little discussion of how nationalisation served the interests of the economy as a whole, and no attempts were made to impose new controls over private industry (**7**, **44**). Labour's much-vaunted National Investment Council was scrapped, and the 1948 Monopolies Act was cautious in its attitude towards restrictive practices. Its major objective – as with much of the Chancellor's policy – was to encourage improved relations between government, employers and workers as the best means of building industrial confidence (**54**). Notwithstanding government rhetoric, the reality was that against the backdrop of the Cold War, controls over the economy were becoming less identified with wartime efficiency and more with the totalitarian methods of East European states. To the dismay of the Labour left in Parliament, the idea of physical control socialist planning, so central to the 1945 programme, was quietly abandoned (**31**). Instead, the government increasingly relied upon demand management* by fiscal and budgetary means, though the extent to which the post-war Treasury committed itself to a 'Keynesian revolution' in economic policy-making remains questionable (**42, 60**).

Industrial policy was also the subject of redefinition after 1947. In the first place, doubts about the value and purpose of nationalisation became more widespread. Resistance to government legislation on iron and steel, finally introduced in 1948, was such that it was agreed to delay implementation of the measure until 1951. Gallup found that twice as many people interviewed opposed as supported this latest measure of public ownership, and party leaders were aware that newly nationalised industries were already becoming targets for alleged lack of profitability and poor industrial relations (**7, 43**). With the Chancellor placing his emphasis on co-operation with private industry in order to boost export production, his Cabinet colleagues became increasingly lukewarm about the idea of drawing up a new shopping list to extend public ownership. Iron and steel began to appear as an end point rather than a staging post, again much to the annoyance of the Labour left (**29, 31**). The government's relations with organised labour similarly underwent modification with Cripps at the Treasury. Rapidly rising wages intensified the Chancellor's concern that inflation would blight the prospects for economic progress, and in 1948 he moved towards the introduction of a wage restraint policy. The TUC leadership, anxious to remain on good terms with the government, officially backed such an approach, but one of the consequences was to usher in a period of growing tension in industrial relations. Union leaders were themselves powerless to prevent localised 'unofficial' stoppages, such as the protracted London dock strike of 1949, and pressure from ordinary members was such that the TUC felt compelled to modify its stance on wage restraint in 1950. Wages and trade unionism, in other words, were rapidly becoming a central ingredient in the national economic dilemma (**36, 56**).

In the short term, the firm resolve of Cripps appeared to be paying off. His concentration on exports produced a particularly striking turn-around in the balance of payments; Britain's deficit on current payments was running at 630 million pounds in 1947, but this fell to only 30 million pounds the following year. In the summer of 1949, however, the economy once more ran into problems. A mild recession in the United States was followed by another 'dollar drain' from Britain, compounded by speculation on the part of dealers against sterling in the foreign-currency markets. The run on the reserves, together with the fall of the pound, threatened a slide into recession, and parallels were soon being drawn with 1947. Cripps, like Dalton, suffered under the strain of events; the Chancellor retired temporarily to a Swiss sanatorium after falling ill, thereby contributing to a lack of clear leadership at a moment of renewed crisis. In his absence, government policy was co-ordinated by three young ministers with strong economic credentials: Douglas Jay, Hugh Gaitskell and Harold Wilson. All three concluded that the only viable means of boosting Britain's reserves was to devalue the pound. This was initially opposed by a majority of the Cabinet, who believed that devaluation would be seen as a symbol of failure on the international stage. But as the dollar drain accelerated, Attlee and his senior colleagues relented. From his sick-bed, Cripps gave weary agreement to a 30-per-cent devaluation, which came into force in September 1949; the exchange rate was thus adjusted from $4.03 to $2.80 to the pound. In spite of criticism that the scale of devaluation was greater than necessary, political opinion generally accepted that drastic action was unavoidable, and indeed ministers could point to some early benefits. The drain on the reserves was rapidly checked, and by the end of 1949 economic indicators, notably exports, were again becoming more favourable (**20**, **45**).

The devaluation crisis, though short-lived, served to reinforce the cautious approach of Cripps to welfare expenditure — another illustration of policy refinement after 1947. As the dollar drain proceeded, the Treasury took the lead in arguing that devaluation would only be effective if accompanied by fresh austerity measures on the home front. This line was strongly opposed by Aneurin Bevan and by Hugh Dalton, who had now returned to government in the role of elder statesman as Chancellor of the Duchy of Lancaster. Freed from the constraints of high office, Dalton was even more categoric than he had been as Chancellor of the Exchequer that welfare reform should not simply be discharged as ballast whenever the economy hit rough water (**101**). Hence the summer of 1949 saw some of the most acrimonious Cabinet meetings chaired by Attlee. Bevan threatened to resign if there were major reductions in social services; Ernest Bevin promised similar action if defence suffered; and Cripps — according to the Prime Minister — was 'ready to resign about anything' (**95**). By late October a compromise agreement had been reached, including minor economies in defence, a cutback in the housing programme and a ceiling on future food subsidies. The most symbolically potent of the post-devaluation announcements, though, concerned the National Health Service, the cost of which was escalating rapidly. The Minister of Health had initially been adamant that any introduction of fees, however limited, would undermine the central principle of a free service. After some hard talking, he accepted the idea of prescription charges in principle, but only on the condition that such charges would not be implemented for the foreseeable future (**63**). The question of health-service charges was thus left in the air, and Cripps – who had hoped to save some 300 million pounds – had to settle for a new package that yielded savings of only 120 million pounds (**20**). Not for the first or last time, there were those who thought the Chancellor had given too much ground to his old friend Bevan.

External, economic forces were not alone in dictating a change in government style after 1947. On the domestic scene, Labour was faced with an increasingly revitalised parliamentary opposition. As Conservatives sought to recover from the shock of the 1945 defeat, Churchill and his senior associates were little match for Attlee's front-bench team in the early days. The failure to make any headway in by-elections prompted a reorganisation of party machinery, aimed at boosting membership and reviving constituency activity; it also assisted those who favoured a fundamental reassessment of domestic policy. Despite Churchill's lacklustre approach, progressives in the Tory ranks, led by the former Education Minister R. A. Butler, managed to incorporate in the Industrial Charter* of 1947 a broad commitment to Keynesian-style demand management* within the mixed economy (**11, 28**). From 1947 onwards, Conservatives also found a populist message: scarcities and shortages, it was alleged, were all due to socialist 'bureaucracy' and 'inefficiency'. The dividends gradually became apparent in electoral terms. Opinion polls showed the parties as neck-and-neck, and by-elections after 1947 showed a consistent swing away from the government (**6, 7**). The effectiveness of the Conservative revival should not be exaggerated. Organisational and policy changes were not sufficient, for example, to deliver actual by-election victories, even in promising constituencies. But the Opposition could no longer be treated with measured disdain in the 'Cripps era', as it had been in Dalton's time at the Treasury. Rather, the Conservative recovery was an additional constraint upon the government; one which figured increasingly in the minds of ministers as they began to prepare for the forthcoming general election.

Planning for the election revealed some sharp divisions in Labour ranks. Herbert Morrison, Chairman of the NEC's* Policy and Publicity Sub-committee, gave a lead to those in favour of consolidation – the idea of presenting a moderate image based upon digesting and improving reforms already introduced. His public speeches focused more and more on the needs of middle-class, suburban and rural voters; to ignore their real difficulties, Morrison claimed, would be 'suicidal' (**25**). This was a barely concealed attack upon colleagues who used more intemperate language. Shinwell's claim that he did not give 'two hoots' for anyone except the working class was used by hostile newspapers to illustrate Labour's continued 'extremism'. Above all, Aneurin Bevan had angered senior colleagues, and received a rebuke from the Prime Minister, for his notorious pronouncement during one speech that Tories were 'lower than vermin' (**95**). Bevan nevertheless emerged as the champion of those who favoured 'advance' rather than consolidation as the centrepiece of the party's electoral strategy. The tension between consolidators and radicals, which had been an underlying theme of Cabinet debates on the iron and steel industry, came more into the open at Labour's annual conference in 1949. Bevan made a strong appeal to socialist idealism, and argued that only further extensive nationalisation would secure public control of the commanding heights of the economy (**31, 92**). Morrison's response, which won overwhelming conference support, was that future nationalisation proposals must be closely related to improving industrial efficiency, and that Labour must be seen not as a 'narrow party', but as 'the party of all the useful people' (**91**).

Morrison won the argument on caution ahead of innovation, though he was less successful in determining the timing of the 1950 election. He alone wanted a delay until the summer, but Cripps made the case that economic prospects might deteriorate and that he could not, in all conscience, introduce a blatantly electioneering budget in the spring. In the event, Attlee settled on February 1950, and the party concentrated on combining Morrisonian appeals to the middle ground with Crippsian calls for increased production (**20**). In contrast to 1945, Labour's campaign looked as much to the past as to the future, emphasising that the post-war settlement would be threatened by the return of Churchill [**doc. 13**]. The Conservatives, for their part, played down the importance of their leader as a personality, and focused instead on the message that they accepted the broad outlines of Britain's welfare state. In the constituencies, candidates of all parties made much of their determination to maintain full employment, with the result that the campaign remained low-key throughout. Careful preparation ensured that the whole thing followed 'an unusually predetermined course. The ambushes and feints were few' (**23**). But if the 1950 campaign was, according to Churchill, 'demure', it was not characterised by apathy on the part of the elaborate. The turnout – 84 per cent of those eligible to vote – was unprecedentedly high, and helped to ensure that Labour polled more votes even than it had in 1945. But so too did the Conservatives, whose recovery was now confirmed. When the results were announced, Labour had secured 315 parliamentary seats, compared to 298 for the Conservatives and 9 for the Liberals. Over the country as a whole, there had been a swing against the government of 2.9 per cent, and Labour was left with a majority of just 6 seats in the House of Commons.

Aside from the redrawing of constituency boundaries, which was estimated to have cost the government 30 seats, the regional pattern of results offered the clearest explanation of this narrow Labour victory. Broadly working-class constituencies, especially in the north and west, remained solidly behind the government. Indeed fifty of the sixty biggest majorities in the country came in Labour strongholds. This helps to explain – with each overwhelming victory producing only one MP – why a clear superiority in numbers of votes cast was not translated into a larger overall majority. On the other hand, Labour clearly lost ground in the areas that had caused ministers most anxiety: constituencies with a preponderance of middle-class voters, both in the suburban districts of towns and cities and in the countryside. In London and the Home Counties especially, the swing to the Conservatives was well above the national average. The implication here was not lost on commentators: whereas Labour's traditional supporters had drawn comfort from full employment and the introduction of new welfare reforms, notably the health service, many more affluent voters were frustrated by continuing restrictions. It was subsequently calculated that the percentage of working-class voters backing Labour had remained constant between 1945 and 1950; but the proportion of the middle-class electorate still loyal to the government had fallen from 21 per cent to 16 per cent (**7, 23**). 'We proclaimed a just policy of "fair shares", reflected Hugh Dalton, 'but the complaint was not so much that shares were unfair, but that they were too small' (**90**).

Looking back on the 1950 election, many on the Labour side agreed that austerity was the primary cause of voters' disaffection. Others, more critical, were inclined to blame the whole drift of policy under Cripps, which, it was alleged, had betrayed the hopes of 1945. Certainly the policy adjustments of the Cripps era – combined with Conservative acceptance of the post-war settlement – had led to a blurring of party distinctions, and left Labour with a much less distinct image. Consensus politics, in other words, originated not so much in the Second World War or its immediate aftermath, but in a mutual convergence towards the political middle ground after 1947 (**14**). Those who depict the retreat to consensus by ministers as a betrayal of socialism tend to underestimate the scale of Labour's achievement. In spite of an unfavourable economic background, high levels of employment had been maintained and Britain's balance-of-payments position was moving back towards equilibrium by 1950 (**45**). Above all, the rhetoric of restraint had not prevented a continued emphasis on welfare expenditure, as those who worked most closely with Cripps were later to testify [**doc. 14**]. If the grim realities of rationing, and unsatisfied material expectations, had alienated some voters, then this has to be set against the increased number of votes cast for Labour overall in 1950; a reflection of the belief, especially amongst ordinary working people, that the government had done its best to build a 'land fit for heroes'. The Cripps era, we might conclude, did not betray the hopes of 1945, though by the same token it offered little that was new or exciting for the future. Under the pressure of events, ministers had increasingly focused their attention on the defence rather than the development of the post-war settlement, a tendency reinforced by the narrowness of the election victory in 1950. This time, unlike 1945, there were no joyous celebrations [**doc. 15**]. Rather, as Attlee's ageing Cabinet was reconstituted in February 1950, the overriding concern was not with what might now be achieved; it was with how long the new government could survive.

7 The Second Attlee Administration

The omens were not good for Labour in February 1950. In forming his new administration, the Prime Minister could still count on the loyalty of an experienced Cabinet. Attlee's senior colleagues – Bevin, Cripps and Morrison – all returned to their posts for the time being; and the small number of ministerial changes made after the election continued to reflect the balance of party forces. Promotion went primarily to reliable figures from the moderate wing of the party, such as James Griffiths, who was rewarded for his work at National Insurance with the Colonial Office, and Hugh Gaitskell, who became the Chancellor's deputy as Minister for Economic Affairs. But the Cabinet, though at the outset harmonious, was acutely aware of the constraints imposed by a tiny parliamentary majority; as one party official put it, the 'tidal wave' of 1945 had receded (**25**). In these changed circumstances, ministers found it difficult to look forward with optimism. The first meeting of the new Cabinet agreed that there was no prospect of introducing any of the controversial legislation outlined in the election manifesto, such as further measures of nationalisation. Any attempt to carry major reforms, it was felt, would result either in debilitating delaying tactics by the House of Lords or the need for an embarrassing retreat if unanimous party support was not forthcoming (**20**). According to Hugh Dalton, who now became Minister of Town and Country Planning, the election result was the worst of all possible outcomes, for it left Labour in office but 'without authority or power'. Indeed, most ministers believed that the government, unable to take strong executive action, would not last for more than six months (**102**). In the event, the second Attlee administration was to remain in office for eighteen months. But the end product was not only electoral defeat in 1951, and the return of the Conservatives to untrammelled power; it was also a profound split in Labour ranks that was to haunt the party throughout the 1950s.

For several months after the election, it seemed that ministerial pessimism might be unwarranted. The first half of 1950 brought a period of sustained economic development. Exports continued to grow at record levels, leading to a much healthier balance-of-payments position; industrial production had increased by 30 per cent over three years; unemployment and the cost of living were under control; and gold and dollars were flowing into the reserves. Indeed, by the end of the year Britain was able to announce that it no longer required the assistance of Marshall Aid (**7**, **45**). This upturn in economic fortunes inevitably made life easier for the government. Opinion polls continued to reflect the result of the general election, and Labour held on to two marginal seats at by-elections in the spring of 1950. Back-benchers also remained in defiant mood. Angered by Conservative attempts at harassment through the use of tiring, all-night sessions, Labour MPs closed ranks and made government defeats in the House of Commons a rarity (**20**). Cabinet unity was threatened in April by one serious disagreement: over the recurring problem of how to control health-service costs. Cripps now sought to impose charges on dentures and spectacles, but found the Minister of Health still strongly opposed to any departure from the principle of a free system, which he said would be 'a grave disappointment to Socialist opinion throughout the world'. After several heated meetings, a compromise was reached whereby Bevan accepted a high ceiling for NHS expenditure in return for the establishment of a Cabinet committee under Attlee to oversee future plans. This formula left unresolved the question of health-service charges, though to outward appearances the Cabinet had papered over any disagreement (**63**). Above all, ministers were buoyed up by economic growth, which held out the prospect of being able to continue in office for longer than anticipated. 'It looks as though those bastards can stay in as long as they like,' Churchill complained after losing one particularly close vote in the Commons (**20**).

In June 1950, however, the government's composure was suddenly upset by an unexpected external development – the Korean War. News of the North Korean attack across the 38th parallel brought a swift response in both Washington and London. The Cabinet, with only Bevan dissenting, was strongly in favour of backing American resistance to North Korean aggression; to allow a blatant violation of international law by Communist forces, it was felt, would be to repeat the folly of 1930s appeasement. As a result, British forces were soon playing their part in the Far East. Initially, Labour's rank-and-file were almost wholly in support of the government. But by the autumn, the mood had changed. This was partly due to the way in which the Korean War unfolded. Instead of confining United Nations forces to a defence of South Korea, the American commander, General MacArthur, led an assault which threatened to escalate hostilities by bringing Communist China into the conflict. Indications that the Americans were now considering the use of atomic weapons caused particularly grave concern among Labour supporters, and indeed the Prime Minister was sufficiently alarmed to make a special visit to Washington in December 1950. Attlee returned triumphantly with assurances from President Truman that atomic weapons would not be used, but back-bench opinion became increasingly concerned that Britain was tying itself inextricably to the aims of American foreign policy (**31**). The clearest indication of this came in January 1951, when the Cabinet agreed to a massive increase in Britain's defence budget. By agreeing to a programme of 4,700 million pounds over the next three years, ministers imposed a heavier burden of defence spending per capita than even the Americans were prepared to contemplate. The result was to be an intense strain on the British economy, necessitating a major redefinition of priorities on the home front.

The task of working out the full implications of the rearmament programme fell primarily to a new Chancellor of the Exchequer, Hugh Gaitskell. In the autumn of 1950 Stafford Cripps was forced to resign through ill-health. The Prime Minister had little doubt that Gaitskell, having served an apprenticeship as deputy to Cripps, was best equipped for the Treasury (**95**). News of the appointment was not, however, universally welcomed in Labour ranks. In particular, Aneurin Bevan felt his record as Minister of Health was sufficient to justify promotion to high office, and he bitterly resented being passed over in favour of someone with no Cabinet experience. There was no doubt a strong element of personal rivalry between the two men; by 1950 they were both regarded as possible future leaders of the party. Gaitskell had already acquired a reputation for economic expertise and administrative competence, though as yet he lacked any strong base of party support outside Westminster. The new Chancellor, Bevan noted contemptuously, was still 'young in the Movement', having entered Parliament only five years earlier. Bevan, by contrast, was one of the darlings of the constituency activists, renowned for his oratorical skills on the public stage; he was, though, less popular with senior colleagues, who regarded him as a temperamental egotist, often unwilling to accept majority Cabinet opinion (**90**, **101**). Over and above personality differences, there were strong disagreements on policy which soon left Gaitskell and Bevan at loggerheads. On his first day at the Treasury, Gaitkell told the Prime Minister that increases in defence spending could only be met if economies were made on domestic services, including the health service. The scene was set for what became, in the spring of 1951, 'a fight for the soul of the Labour Party' [**doc. 16**].

In preparing his first budget, the Chancellor made provision for the imposition of new charges for dentures and spectacles. On 22 March the Cabinet, chaired by Herbert Morrison during Attlee's absence in hospital, agreed with Gaitskell that charges were unavoidable, given the need for domestic economies. Bevan, although now serving as Minister of Labour, repeated his objections to such a course: he argued that Labour was committed to defending the social services, and that any required economies should be sought in the 'inflated' defence programme. Shortly afterwards, he aroused press speculation about Cabinet rifts by declaring in public that he would not remain a member of a government that departed from the principle of a free health service. Last-minute attempts to find a compromise came to nothing. The day before the budget, ministers – after hearing a counter threat of resignation from Gaitskell if forced to retreat – reaffirmed their commitment to introducing charges. Attlee, from his hospital bed, had tried to warn of the likely electoral consequences of a government split, but ultimately agreed that the Chancellor must prevail. Hence on 10 April Gaitskell went ahead in announcing new charges as one element of a generally well-received budget. After listening to pleas from several sources, Bevan did not resign immediately, but continued to insist in Cabinet that he could not vote for the new measures. Further attempts at compromise were undermined by a stinging attack in the Labour newspaper *Tribune*, claiming that Gaitskell had 'sold out' to the Tories [**doc. 17**]. In response to Attlee's injunction that he must now accept collective responsibility for Cabinet decisions, Bevan finally went ahead with his resignation on 22 April, to be followed shortly afterwards by two more junior members of the government – Harold Wilson and John Freeman. Freed from the constraints of office, Bevan made violent accusations against his former colleagues, first in the House of Commons and then at a stormy meeting of the parliamentary party; many press commentators now delighted in speaking of a divided administration and a 'Bevanite' challenge to the leadership (**20, 63**).

The causes and implications of this first major split in Labour ranks since 1945 have been much debated. Health-service charges were clearly symbolic of a deep division about the future direction of the Labour movement. Bevan was convinced that 'Hugh is a Tory', prepared to abandon socialist principles for the sake of electoral respectability; for his part, Gaitskell believed that unless checked, Bevan would break Labour just as Lloyd George had broken the Liberal Party (**87, 102**). These passionately held views have coloured subsequent historical judgements. Bevan's first biographer presented the episode as a conspiracy by the Chancellor, deliberately aimed at forcing Bevan's resignation; defenders of Gaitskell have argued that it was Bevan who behaved erratically – seeking to make the health service a sacred cow at a time when other spending departments accepted the need for economies (**34, 92, 107**). On a personal level, both men can clearly be faulted. Gaitskell showed a streak of inflexibility which surprised even his closest supporters, some of whom advised him that the relatively small amount of savings envisaged was not worth the trouble caused (**96**). As for Bevan, his increasingly strident behaviour eventually alienated some of those who sympathised with his aims; as one minister commented, it was intolerable for Cabinet majorities of eighteen to two to be overturned just because Bevan happened to be one of the two. Indeed, the violence of Bevan's language after his resignation strengthened a widespread impression in the party that he had become an impossible colleague (**107**). Solely in terms of the issues involved, however, events were subsequently to bear out much of Bevan's case. A last-minute rush to obtain spectacles and false teeth while they were still free offset the level of savings envisaged, and more seriously, production difficulties made it impossible to carry out fully the rearmament programme agreed by the Cabinet. 'Perhaps Bevan, with all his faults', concludes his less sympathetic biographer, John Campbell, 'was worth £13 million after all' (**88**).

The legacy of the dispute over health-service charges clouded the remaining months of Attlee's administration. After his resignation outbursts, Bevan himself was generally restrained in his criticism of the government, though some of his supporters were more forthright. The 'Bevanites' were still as yet a small and shifting group of MPs, but with the potential to make embarrassingly public attacks on Gaitskell's economic policy and the rearmament programme. In *Keeping Left*, for example, disaffected back-benchers criticised the whole concept of consolidation, and argued – contrary to ministerial wishes – in favour of industrial democracy within a greatly expanded nationalisation programme (**31**). Such criticisms served to compound the difficulties facing the government in the summer of 1951. The Chancellor in particular struggled with problems that had beset his predecessor: a sudden deterioration in the balance of payments, a mounting dollar deficit and inflationary wage pressures. Gaitskell sought to rally party opinion with some radical initiatives, such as the proposal to limit company dividends in return for wage restraint, but higher taxes following the budget made it difficult to avoid the conclusion that rearmament was adversely affecting all sectors of the economy (**45**).

Nor could much comfort be drawn from the government's foreign policy. The pressures on Ernest Bevin finally took their toll in 1951; he was forced to leave the Foreign Office through ill-health in the spring, and died whilst the Cabinet were wrangling over health-service charges. Within the space of six months, the Prime Minister had thus lost his two most able servants, Cripps and Bevin, with disastrous consequences for the government. Aside from the effects on domestic policy, Bevin's death left a void in foreign affairs that was difficult to fill. After considering the claims of Bevan, whose sense of frustration was heightened by being passed over again for high office, Attlee decided that the post of Foreign Secretary should go to Herbert Morrison, on grounds of seniority if nothing else. But Morrison was soon regarded as a pale imitation of Bevin; a man whose mind, in the words of one critic, had not ranged beyond the sound of Bow Bells. Although there was an element of Foreign Office snobbery in much of the criticism, it remained the case that Morrison became bogged down in a series of complex disputes: over Britain's relationship with Iran and Egypt, over German rearmament, and over the Korean War, which continued without sign of resolution (**21**, **91**). Taken together, domestic and foreign policy left an impression of a government with little sense of direction. Conservative back-benchers, sensing that they had ministers on the run, redoubled their efforts to demoralise Labour with late-night sittings in the Commons. The Opposition could also take comfort from electoral indicators: by September 1951, opinion polls showed a clear 10-per-cent lead for the Conservatives (**4**).

In these circumstances, it came as a surprise when Attlee announced the dissolution of Parliament and a fresh general election in October. The Prime Minister's decision was prompted, at least in part, by his concern that the King was scheduled to visit Australia the following spring; it would be unfair, Attlee felt, that he should go away with the threat of a 'political crisis' hanging over him (**25**). This constitutional propriety did not impress other senior ministers, such as Morrison and Gaitskell, who believed a delay would allow time for an economic recovery. Once the campaign was under way, however, all sections of the party sought to leave behind recent troubles. Aneurin Bevan spoke out strongly in favour of party unity, and could take comfort from some radical proposals in Labour's manifesto, such as suggestions for a limited levy on capital and advances towards the introduction of comprehensive secondary schools (**20**). Aside from these items, the general tone of the manifesto – as in 1950 – was one of consolidation. The government again stressed the need to preserve post-war advances, such as full employment and the welfare state; nationalisation was further relegated as a priority by Labour promising only to act in the case of industries 'failing the nation'. The Conservative campaign also followed the pattern of the previous year: a Churchill government, it was claimed, would develop welfare reform – by building more houses, in particular – and would 'set the people free' from socialist controls and bureaucracy (**4**). The continued narrowing of party differences on domestic policy made for a generally low-key campaign. Conservatives sought hard to exploit Labour divisions, inventing the slogan 'The End is Nye' – implying that the disruption associated with Bevan meant that the government's days were numbered. Herbert Morrison also tried to enliven proceedings in the few days before the poll by describing Churchill as a warmonger. But political commentators were agreed that the sharp animosity of 1945 was lacking; many newspapers had to resort to detailed descriptions of Mrs Attlee's eccentric driving, as the Prime Minister busied himself with crossword puzzles in the back of his car on a nationwide tour.

The result of the election was a narrow Conservative victory, bringing Churchill back to power to form his first peacetime administration. On an average swing of 0.9 per cent, the Tories made twenty-three gains, winning a total of 321 seats, compared with 295 for Labour. The great majority of the electorate, according to polling evidence, voted the same way as in 1950; for the small, but decisive, number who did switch allegiance, increases in the cost of living had proved the most crucial consideration (**7**). The clash between Gaitskell and Bevan had clearly not helped Labour's cause, though the importance of rising prices and unsatisfied material expectations was reflected in the regional pattern of results. Over half the Conservative gains were made in the south-east, in constituencies such as Dulwich and Camberwell, where Churchill's rallying cry offering prosperity and opportunity had its greatest appeal (**4**). There were several ironies about the 1951 result. In the first place, George VI's sudden death compounded Attlee's tactical error in calling for an early election; during 1952 the British economy entered a phase of steady growth from which Labour might well have benefited had they remained longer in office [**doc. 18**]. In addition, Labour had actually won more votes, though fewer seats, than the Conservatives; the total of nearly 14 million votes cast for Labour was the largest ever recorded in British politics. As a consequence, party stalwarts were by no means downcast at the result. For senior figures such as Hugh Dalton, there was relief at being released from the burden of almost a decade in high office. In contrast to his gloom in 1950, Dalton described the outcome in 1951 as 'wonderful', believing that the Conservatives would soon run into electoral difficulties (**102**). In the event, he was to be profoundly mistaken. Most of Labour's generation of 1945 were never again to return to government; by 1952, fierce factional in-fighting was under way between consolidators and radicals, or Gaitskellites and Bevanites as they became known. It was not until 1964, thirteen years after Attlee's departure, that another Labour Prime Minister was to enter Downing Street.

Part Three: Assessment

The Attlee governments have no shortage of detractors. In 1951 one senior civil servant concluded that the experience of the previous six years 'puts me in mind of nothing so much as the voyage of Columbus in 1492. You will recall that when Columbus set out he didn't know where he was going; when he arrived he didn't know where he was; and when he returned he didn't know where he had been' (**59**). According to many subsequent critics, Labour's 'ship of state' was, at best, heading in the wrong direction. Commentators on the political right have attacked the post-war government for introducing too much socialism. The emphasis on welfare reform, in particular, diverted attention from desperately needed industrial regeneration, and the principle of universal benefits, as opposed to pre-war selectivity, was undesirable both financially and morally (**9**, **40**). This line of reasoning, however, shows scant recognition of the historical context that gave rise to Attlee's administration. Labour's landslide victory in 1945 was rooted, as we have seen, in cynicism about the record and intentions of Churchill's Conservative Party. After six years of privation and grim resistance in wartime, there was a great desire – both among civilians at home and service personnel abroad – to ensure that British society was changed swiftly and radically; a determination that promises of improved social provision must this time be honoured, and 'never again' abandoned as they had been by successive Conservative-dominated governments after the First World War. Churchill's cool attitude to the whole process of reconstruction after 1943 only served to deepen the view that what Conservativism offered was an old recipe – jam tomorrow (**14**). Against this background, the desire of the post-war government to remedy social inequality was entirely understandable; Labour was elected in 1945 precisely because of its commitment to measures that the British people felt had too long been denied.

The major complaint of left-wing critics, nevertheless, has been that the Attlee years did not see enough socialism. Labour ministers, it has been argued, may have introduced long-overdue social reforms, but they failed to redistribute wealth or to break down rigid class barriers; 1 per cent of the population, for example, still owned 50 per cent of all private capital (**18, 30**). Much of this critique, however, suffers from being constructed too readily with the benefit of hindsight. The continued existence of poverty and social inequality, in spite of the welfare state, was much easier to gauge in the 1950s; in other words, only after the 1945 reforms became operational and Labour had left office. Nor was it the case that ministers were deliberately shunning the implementation of a more radical programme. By the admission of all historians, the Labour left after 1945 was 'uncertain of its aims, confused about methods and weak in numbers' (**29**). This reflected not only a sense of loyalty stemming from acknowledgement of government successes, but also an inability to devise coherent alternative policies (**31**). The Keep Left group and other disaffected MPs themselves paid little attention in the immediate post-war years to social questions such as poverty, housing and health; and where more radical ideas were floated – as in the case of urging workers' control in industry – detailed plans for implementation were rarely forthcoming. Those who pressed at the time for 'more socialism' were, in short, imprecise about what this would mean in practice.

Clearly any government can be criticised for not going far enough, and for those hoping to see the elimination of capitalism, Attlee's ministry proved to be profoundly disappointing. But when judged against a range of contemporary yardsticks – the performance of previous governments, the aims of Labour compared with the Conservative Party, and the economic circumstances inherited in 1945 – Attlee's record emerges in a far more positive light. What then might be regarded as the major achievements of these years? In the first place, the government could claim credit for its part in the nation's post-war economic recovery. By the end of the war, as we have seen, British export trade had been decimated and foreign assets had disappeared. Over the next six years, Attlee's Cabinet provided the circumstances necessary for sustained – if at times erratic – economic growth, as measured by a variety of performance indicators. There was a threefold increase in export volume; industrial output grew by one-third; and the gross domestic product rose by 3 per cent per year after 1947. With the assistance of the American loan and Marshall Aid*, the balance of payments showed current-account surpluses in 1948 and 1950, before the Korean War led to a deficit in 1951. And in spite of rising import costs, consumer prices and wage rates were pegged to average rises of less than 5 per cent. All this measured favourably with the record of successive governments before the war (**45**).

Perhaps most notable of all in economic terms, unemployment – with the temporary exception of 1947 – had been kept at far lower levels than between the wars. Though the resumption of world trade, by releasing suppressed wartime demand, had much to do with this, it would be wrong to underestimate the role of ministerial policy. The same circumstances, after all, applied at the end of the First World War, when market forces produced a short-term boom followed by a deep recession. Careful planning after 1945 helped to ensure first that demobilisation was carried out without upsetting economic recovery, and secondly that there was no return to high unemployment in the pre-war depressed regions of northern and western Britain. Unemployment throughout the north-east coastal region in 1938 had been 38 per cent; in June 1951 it was running at 1.5 per cent (**13**). The most exhaustive study of Labour's economic policy concludes that it was difficult to see how this performance could have been improved upon; these were years when – contrary to the claim of the civil servant speaking in 1951 – 'the government knew where it wanted to go and led the country with an understanding of what was at stake' (**45**).

Economic recovery was the essential foundation of Labour's welfare programme. Again, this might best be judged in terms of the improvements made, in the face of considerable resistance, over pre-war provision. The long list of legislative reforms carried through the House of Commons provided, in the final analysis, services of a kind that had hitherto been unthinkable for those of modest means. Aside from the security of employment which came with economic recovery – itself unknown for millions before 1939 – Labour's programme offered fresh hope and opportunity. For the young, free secondary education became a right for the first time; for the elderly, old-age pensions approximated as never before to the level of a living income. Bevan's house-building programme meant that affordable, decent accommodation was, as never before, within the reach of thousands of lower-income families. And this was without the most popular of Labour's reforms, the National Health Service, which in its first year of operation treated some 8.5 million dental patients and dispensed more than 5 million pairs of spectacles, illustrating the pent-up demand that existed within British society for medical services (**32**). If, as critics claim, relations between the sexes were not fundamentally altered, nevertheless working-class women could now benefit from a range of new services: family allowances, improved opportunities at school, and free health care. One woman later recalled how, on the evening before the health service came into operation, she was delivered of her baby shortly before midnight. The next morning she was presented with a bill for £6 by the doctor; had the baby been born fifteen minutes later, there would have been no charge (**37**). This was what most Labour supporters understood by socialism in practice.

On the world stage, the government could point to a string of achievements: the forging of the Anglo-American special relationship, upon which Western security was henceforth to be based; the emergence of a democratic Germany; and the initiation of moves towards independence for a considerable proportion of the world's colonial population. Subsequent claims that Bevin should have done more to prepare for Britain's eclipse as a world power, though easy to make with hindsight, again ignore the realities of 1945. In spite of the inexorable rise of the superpowers, Britain was still a major military and industrial power at the end of the war, and thus had every reason to proceed cautiously in reviewing global commitments. As for missing the opportunity to create a European 'third force', it must be remembered that only a quarter of Britain's trade in the late 1940s was with the European mainland; politicians and officials alike had no reason for thinking that the Commonwealth and the so-called Sterling Area would not remain predominant in trading terms (**65, 78**). The idea that Britain had overstretched itself only came to have greater validity in the 1950s, after the economic importance of Western Europe became more obvious and events such as Suez highlighted the fragility of the British Empire. Bevin's legacy, in the meantime, was that he

> provided his successors with the indispensable basis of security in the Western Alliance on which they could then proceed to make whatever adjustments were necessary and to develop such options as entry into Europe and withdrawal from the Middle East and east of Suez (**84**).

It would of course be misleading to imply that the Labour administration had no shortcomings. There were, as with all governments, avoidable failures. The fuel crisis of 1947, for example, owed much to Shinwell's inability to heed the danger signals about worsening coal shortages. In other instances, the promises of 1945 remained unfulfilled. Labour had retreated on its commitment to economic planning, and there had been increasing disillusionment with nationalisation. While the benefits of some public-service industries, such as transport, were immediately recognisable, it was not clear by 1951 how the nationalisation programme as a whole contributed either to planning or to the ultimate creation of a 'Socialist Commonwealth'. Nor had the government, with its over-riding emphasis on export-led recovery, got to grips with some of the underlying weaknesses of the economy, such as an excessive reliance on overmanned staple industries, though again it was only in later years that the main features of the 'British industrial disease' came to be recognised (**36**). Some aspects of Bevin's foreign policy were also regarded at the time as indefensible, and not only by those who were disappointed that Labour did not bring a fresh approach to the harsh world of power politics. A case in point here was the government's benign attitude towards South Africa, which was an important market for British exports and a key source of the uranium necessary to develop nuclear weapons. When one junior minister urged a stiffening of British policy, in view of the racist nature of the South African regime, he was promptly dismissed from office and his views ignored (**20**).

These failings did not, though, seriously detract from the government's achievements across the board. More important, at least to the subsequent development of the Labour Party, were two further difficulties, each left unresolved at the time of the 1951 election. In the first place, Labour became the victim of its own success. Implementation of the party's domestic programme, painstakingly drawn up over many years, left an obvious problem: what was to be Labour's new vision of the future? This question inevitably became entangled with tactical considerations, as well as raising issues of ideology and principle. For the likes of Morrison, consolidation of gains made since 1945 was the essential priority; only a moderate Labour Party, it was argued, could remain attractive to broad sections of the electorate. Middle-class voters especially, if recent electoral evidence was to be believed, were increasingly concerned not with the fading wartime ethos of fair shares, but with the material affluence that might result from economic growth. Many other activists, however, felt that consolidation on its own was insufficient for a party that had always been committed to radical change. Strenuous efforts should therefore be made to fill the void created by the fulfilment of Labour's traditional programme. The party, as some of its supporters were soon to argue:

> is in urgent need of a theoretical critique which can serve to
> generate a new dynamic sufficient to carry its members to the

outskirts of the Socialist Commonwealth. No longer can it gain victory taking a stand against the evils and iniquities of laisser-faire capitalism, for they have long been abolished by the Welfare State. The mixed economy itself is now the point of departure and it is difficult to imagine any further evolution of socialist politics that does not subject the Welfare State to an analysis as searching as that which the Webbs directed at the capitalism of their day (**59**).

This problem, of tensions inherent in constructing a programme appropriate for the 1950s, was closely linked with a second difficulty: that of the age profile of the party leadership. The task of rein-vigorating Labour policy would clearly rest with the younger members of Attlee's team. But, as we have seen, opportunities for the promotion of talent from the junior ranks had been limited. The senior ministers who dominated Cabinet proceedings were all mem-bers of the same, by now ageing, political generation; their capacity for innovative policy formation increasingly diminished. Morrison, while urging the party to rethink its principles in a world of full employment and clamouring consumerism, was unable to spell out precisely what should be done: the limit of his vision was simply now to 'pause and consolidate' (**91**). The authority of the 'big five' had, in the short term, been the foundation of Labour's achieve-ments after 1945; but it also helped to delay the process of rethinking party strategy. What was worse, the two leading representatives of the younger generation, Bevan and Gaitskell, had split the party asunder before the debate about future priorities had really got under way. Taken together, these two factors – the void at the heart of Labour policy by 1951 and the divisions created by the Bevan–Gaitskell dispute – clouded the legacy of the Attlee years. Labour had not only exhausted its traditional programme; the search for something to put in its place proved to be so damaging that there was unlikely to be any early return to office. Unlike Columbus, we might conclude, Attlee's government knew where it had been, but was much less certain about where it was going. 'This period', in the words of David Howell, 'might have been the party's heroic age, but like many feats of heroism it had a devastating effect on the hero' (**12**).

Part Four: Documents

document 1
Labour's 1945 election manifesto

*The 1945 programme combined both socialist idealism and pragmatic policies,
and differed considerably in tone and emphasis from its Conservative counterpart.*

The nation needs a tremendous overhaul, a great programme of
modernisation and re-equipment of its homes, its factories and
machinery, its schools, its social services.

All parties say so – the Labour Party means it. For the Labour
Party is prepared to achieve it by drastic policies of replanning and
by keeping a firm constructive hand on our whole productive
machinery; the Labour Party will put the community first and the
sectional interests of private business after. . . .

What will the Labour Party do?

First, the whole of the national resources, in land, material and
labour must be fully employed. Production must be raised to the
highest level and related to purchasing power. . . . It is doubtful
whether we have ever, except in war, used the whole of our productive capacity. This must be corrected because, upon our ability to
produce and organise a fair and generous distribution of the product,
the standard of living of our people depends.

Secondly, a high and constant purchasing power can be maintained through good wages, social services and insurance, and
taxation which bears less heavily on the lower-income groups. But
everybody knows that money and savings lose their value if prices
rise, so rents and the prices of the necessities of life will be controlled.

Thirdly, planned investment in essential industries and on houses,
schools, hospitals and civic centres will occupy a large field of capital
expenditure. A National Investment Board will determine social
priorities and promote better timing in private investment. . . . The
location of new factories will be suitably controlled, and where
necessary the Government will itself build factories. There must be
no depressed areas in the New Britain. . . .

Each industry must have applied to it the test of national service. If it serves the nation, well and good; if it is inefficient and falls down on the job, the nation must see that things are put right.

These propositions seem indisputable, but for years before the war anti-Labour Governments set them aside, so that British industry over a large field fell into a state of depression, muddle and decay. Millions of working and middle-class people went through the horrors of unemployment and insecurity. It is not enough to sympathise with these victims: we must develop an acute feeling of national shame – and act.

The Labour Party is a Socialist Party, and proud of it. Its ultimate purpose at home is the establishment of the Socialist Commonwealth of Great Britain – free, democratic, efficient, progressive, public-spirited, its material resources organised in the service of the British people.

Let Us Face the Future: A Declaration of Labour Policy for the Consideration of the Nation, 1945.

document 2
Reaction to the 1945 victory

Labour supporters were surprised and elated as news of the election result came in. Chuter Ede, who served as deputy to the Conservative Education Minister, R. A. Butler, in the wartime coalition, compared events to the Liberal landslide of 1906.

. . . at 12 noon came the staggering announcement: 'The Government hold 24 seats; the Opposition 100. . . .' Bracken, Amery, Grigg, Sandys, Lloyd, Macmillan, Somervell & Hore-Belisha [ministers in Churchill's caretaker government] were all stated to be out. . . . I began to wonder if I should wake up to find it all a dream. The 3 p.m. announcement opened with the statement that Labour now with 364 seats had a clear majority over all others. . . . All Tyneside had voted Socialist. All the Durham County seats had been held & we appeared to have won all the Durham Boroughs. . . . In Greater London there were 32 Labour gains. Manchester returned only one Tory; Birmingham has 3 Tories and 10 Lab. . . .

This is as great as 1906. I warned Butler more than once that one day the nation . . . would swing violently left. I had expected it to be at the election following this but the hatred of the Tories has been so great that they have been swept out of office by a tidal wave. This is one of the unique occasions in British history – a Red Letter day in the best sense of that term. About 9.40 p.m. [it was confirmed] that Churchill had gone to Buckingham Palace, where he had resigned. Attlee had been summoned and had accepted the King's invitation to form a Govt. . . .

As I had often foretold the country desiring to give power to the Left had followed the precedent of 1906 when it installed the steady, faithful but uninspiring Campbell-Bannerman. Attlee is no firework but the country found that Churchill had produced the appropriate background for our Party's set piece. Attlee's speech [to the PLP, two days later] was typical. Without a trace of emotion he alluded to the tremendous nature of our victory. . . . We were not going to postpone bringing in our measures. This session we should submit our programme. This determination moved the gathering to great enthusiasm. . . . The new Party is a great change from the old. It teems with bright, vivacious servicemen. The superannuated Trade Union official seems hardly to be noticeable in the ranks.

K. Jefferys, ed., (**97**): diary entries, 26–28 July 1945, pp. 226–9.

document 3

Attlee as Prime Minister

Douglas Jay, who worked for a short period at No. 10 Downing Street after 1945, was well placed to observe the Prime Minister's qualities, and his particular alliance with Ernest Bevin, the Foreign Secretary.

More complicated characters than Attlee, including Herbert Morrison and Nye Bevan – and even Michael Foot – have found it incomprehensible that such a man could have attained the position he did, and held it for twenty years. 'No one', says Michael Foot, 'has ever unravelled the riddle.' 'It was quite impossible', said Morrison in his autobiography, 'to approach near enough to get into his mind and know what he was really thinking.' The truth, my experience would incline me to judge, was simpler. Attlee was a straightforward Victorian Christian, who believed one should do one's job and one's duty, whether as an Army officer or Member of Parliament or Prime Minister. My own father, though lacking Attlee's capacities, was in character a similar type, and sprang from a similar background; so that the characteristics were not unrecognizable to me. Nor should one suppose that, because this type may now be extinct, it therefore never existed. But secondly Attlee combined in a rare measure the three qualities of honesty, common sense and intelligence: the first two to an outstanding degree and the third on a much higher level than many recognized.

None of Attlee's colleagues in the Government, apart from Bevin, so manifestly possessed all three qualities together; and it was these, as it seemed to me, which enabled him to retain authority over such diverse and explosive individuals as Morrison, Bevin, Dalton, Cripps and Bevan. Attlee's reliability inspired ever-increasing confidence among colleagues. Above all, it endeared him to Bevin. As reported to me at the time, Bevin, after a three-hour barrage from Dalton on a drive back from Durham on 26 July 1947, in support of the foolish Cripps/Dalton plan to replace Attlee by Bevin as PM, responded with the brief words: 'I'm sticking to little Clem.'

Douglas Jay (**96**), p. 135.

document 4

Britain's 'financial Dunkirk'

The advice given by Keynes to ministers highlighted the stark economic realities which faced Britain at the end of the war.

Three sources of financial assistance have made it possible for us to mobilise our domestic man-power for war with an intensity not approached elsewhere, and to spend cash abroad, mainly in India and the Middle East, on a scale not equalled by the Americans, *without having to export* in order to pay for the food and raw materials which we were using at home or to provide the cash which we were spending abroad. . . .

As it is, the more or less sudden drying up of these sources of assistance shortly after the end of the Japanese war will put us in an almost desperate plight, unless some other source of temporary assistance can be found to carry us over whilst we recover our breath – a plight far worse than most people, even in Government Departments, have yet appreciated.

The three sources of financial assistance have been (a) Lend-Lease from the United States; (b) Mutual Aid from Canada; (c) Credits (supplemented by sales of our pre-war capital assets) from the Sterling Area. . . .

It seems . . . that there are three essential conditions without which we have not a hope of escaping what might be described, without exaggeration and without implying that we should not even-tually recover from it, a financial Dunkirk. These conditions are (a) an intense concentration on the expansion of exports, (b) drastic and immediate economies in our overseas expenditure, and (c) substan-tial aid from the United States on terms which we can accept. They can only be fulfilled by a combination of the greatest enterprise, ruthlessness and tact.

What does one mean in this context by 'a financial Dunkirk'? What would happen in the event of insufficient success? That is not easily foreseen. Abroad it would require a sudden and humiliating withdrawal from our onerous responsibilities with great loss of pres-tige and an acceptance for the time being of the position of a second-class Power, rather like the present position of France. . . . At home a greater degree of austerity would be necessary than we have experienced at any time during the war. And there would have to be an indefinite postponement of the realisation of the best hopes of the new Government.

'Our Overseas Financial Prospects', memorandum by Lord Keynes, 13 August 1945: R. Bullen and M. E. Pelly (eds), *Documents on British Policy Overseas*, Series I, Volume III, HMSO, 1987, pp. 28–37.

document 5
Introducing the National Health Service

Bevan's wife, Jennie Lee, pinpointed the competing pressures upon the minister in seeking to establish the new health service.

At a time when [Nye] was locked in endless stormy negotiations with the British Medical Association, the violence of the attacks on him frightened some of his colleagues. They urged that more con-cessions be given to his critics. While cold feet under the Cabinet table were making life difficult for Nye in private, hot-heads, led by the Socialist Medical Association, were lambasting him in public. There must be no concessions – a full-time salaried staff, no private beds – the socialist dream, the whole dream, and nothing but the dream. Nye in private made the same comment about the demands of Dr Stark Murray and his Socialist Medical Association colleagues as he had made about the ILP when it insisted on disaffiliating from the Labour Party – pure but impotent. Sometimes he swore under his breath at the importunities of the purists, but with no real grudge against them. In his philosophical moments he would say it was a good thing he was being pressed by the Socialist Medical Association to make no concessions, as this helped to balance the much more powerful right-wing pressure groups he had to contend with at the same time. He sought always what he called 'the principle of action'. What, he would ask himself, is the maximum I can hope to achieve in these particular circumstances?

Jennie Lee (**98**), p. 177.

document 6

Annus Mirabilis

In spite of economic pressures, ministers such as Dalton, the Chancellor of the Exchequer, could take comfort from the advances made during the early months of the Attlee administration.

For the Labour Government, 1946 was an Annus Mirabilis. We fully maintained our impetus. We enacted a heavy and varied instalment of our programme.

By the end of the 1945–46 session we had passed Acts of Parliament nationalizing the Bank of England, the Coal Industry, Civil Aviation, and Cable and Wireless; two Finance Acts embodying my first and second Budgets, and my Borrowing (Control and Guarantees) Act; a National Insurance Act, substantially increasing pensions and other benefits; a National Insurance (Industrial Injuries) Act; an Act establishing, at one blow and in full plenitude, a National Health Service; a New Towns Act, and a Trade Disputes and Trade Unions Act, a straight repeal of vindictive and objectionable Tory legislation. This was assuredly a record legislative harvest, of which we might feel proud.

In the Labour Party substantial unity continued both in and out of Parliament, except on certain issues of foreign policy. . . . Public support of the Government all through the country continued unabated; so did public interest in Parliamentary proceedings. Sales of *Hansard* soared, and queues of visitors seeking a seat in the public gallery were always long. Parliament was a living and dramatic spectacle, successfully challenging competition with all other forms of entertainment. . . . It was the best British parliamentary year since the war.

Hugh Dalton (**90**), p. 93.

The fuel crisis of 1947

Many observers blamed Shinwell, the Minister of Fuel and Power, for not warning about coal shortages; Shinwell later defended himself by pointing the finger at others.

On 3 January, after a number of submissions to the Cabinet which failed to gain any useful response, I submitted a paper in which I spelled out the facts and figure [*sic*] of the impending crisis. I did not enjoy any constructive response. Barnes, the Minister of Transport, failed to implement my request that the railwaymen be asked to work at weekends to move more than a million tons of coal lying at the pitheads, beyond passing on the suggestion to the unions and requesting them to take notice. Cripps muttered about damage to his export drive. Bevin did not disguise his lack of interest in a problem he considered no concern of his. Only Attlee indicated awareness of the seriousness of the coming crisis, and subsequently he stressed in a public admission that the responsibility was not solely mine but that of the whole Cabinet.

Three weeks later the worst winter of the century began with heavy snow and frost. Drastic measures would have been necessary whatever the situation as regards coal output or reserves at the pithead and power stations. Dumps were frozen solid, coal wharves isolated, power lines down, and movement by rail or road impossible for some weeks. As it was 1,800,000 were temporarily unemployed and an estimated £200 million of exports were allegedly lost. This loss was due largely to Cripps's decision, in mid-January, to cut coal supplies to industry by fifty per cent in order to maintain public electricity supplies. . . .

In retrospect I must admit that I should have told Parliament and the nation the truth, as I did to the Cabinet. The absenteeism in the pits was excessive. Many miners were too old for the work they were given when the coming shortage of coal was obvious. Equipment was outdated. Nationalization would not magically solve these problems; time was needed to get more skilled men and create a better organization. Yet, if I had publicly described these unpalatable truths, it would have been a reflection on the miners; it would have exposed the pretensions of the miners' leaders; and finally it would have been a bitter blow to the party which had advocated nationalization as the solution for all difficulties.

No approval of anything Dalton did in the crisis is possible. He appeared to dislike everyone but himself, his actions always contrived for his own benefit and without regard for his colleagues or his party or indeed the country.

Emanuel Shinwell (**103**), pp. 194–5.

document 8

Economic and political crisis

Like Shinwell over the coal shortage, Herbert Morrison, recalling the crises of July–November 1947, was not afflicted by any sense of personal responsibility.

The 1947 economic crisis was at root largely due to the faulty administration at the Treasury for which Dalton must be held responsible as head of the department. Cripps, who was by this time a close friend of Dalton's, felt that economic co-ordination required the attention of a full-time economic minister. Cripps, with the support of Dalton, was ready to lay the blame at Attlee's feet.

I was told that Cripps wanted Bevin to be prime minister, and that Dalton agreed to this. Bevin, it was said – apparently wrongly – was ready to accept. I was asked what would I do? I have never felt up to indulging in high conspiracy and I refused to participate. Anyway, the conspiracy failed. . . .

Dalton, by a lapse which was in itself silly rather than grave, but had to be regarded as serious, destroyed all chance of fulfilling his high ambitions and soon became a somewhat soured man. . . . Correct in his behaviour and honourable to an extreme, Dalton put all the facts before the PM and offered his resignation. . . . As tended to happen all too often the PM gave no definite lead and meticulously refrained from voicing his own opinion, obligingly murmuring 'yes, yes' or 'no, no' to much the same sort of question according to the answer the questioner seemed to be expecting. . . . Although I had done my best to save him the decision was that Dalton's offer to resign should be accepted. That night Sir Stafford Cripps was made Chancellor of the Exchequer.

Herbert Morrison (**100**), pp. 260–2.

document 9

Annus Horrendus

*If 1946 had been Annus Mirabilis [**doc. 6**], then 1947 brought little joy for the Chancellor of the Exchequer, and culminated in his resignation.*

One of my younger friends, of the 1945 vintage of Labour MPs, once told me, in a jesting mood, that, in the light of my performance during this time, and my popularity particularly among the younger Labour MPs, I might have become Prime Minister, had I not told, when in ebullient mood, so many slightly malicious stories about my Ministerial colleagues. When I asked him in what year this event might have occurred, he said in 1947. I replied that this was not one of my good years, and that, in spite of certain manoeuvres which were known to us both . . . the office of Prime Minister was in no real danger of becoming vacant in that year.

The year 1947 was indeed a black year. My cheap-money drive encountered a stubborn check. There was a fuel crisis and a food shortage. Departmental Ministers carried the can. 'Starve with Strachey and Shiver with Shinwell' was a clever Tory jibe. But much the worst of all, for me, was the intractable unbalance of our external payments, and the much too rapid exhaustion of the United States and Canadian loans, and of our gold and dollar reserves. It was this apparently insoluble problem, and my vain efforts to solve it, which gradually wore me down.

A number of my friends told me afterwards, though they said nothing to discourage me at the time, that, month by month, they saw a growing change in me. I appeared much less gay, though I could still rally in my old style on important occasions. But, more and more, I seemed strained and ill, and it was clear to many that a break might come. One of my friends recalls that I said to him that to watch the continued loss of our reserves was 'like watching a child bleed to death' and being unable to stop it. My resignation from the Treasury in November 1947 followed the so-called 'Budget incident'. . . . Some thought there was a death wish in this incident. But this was not so. I might, no doubt, have resigned earlier, on grounds of health, or asked for an easier office. But this I was much too proud to do.

Hugh Dalton (**90**), pp. 5–6.

Keeping left

Unease within the party about government policy was led by back-bench MPs who formed the Keep Left group, which was particularly critical of the Foreign Secretary.

Looking back at 1946 from this distance it seems quite remarkable that the 1945 hope and expectation of a great leap towards a socialist Britain should have faded so fast that it took only a year to throw up a rebel group. It's difficult to recapture now the deep disappointment and disillusion which afflicted many of the new young Members as we saw our Government moving rapidly away from the Party's socialist philosophy and principles and settling comfortably, as to the manner born, into the welcoming arms of the capitalist Establishment. . . .

We criticised the policies of the Government in other areas besides foreign affairs; there were also Northern Ireland, and conscription, and economic planning. For a year after the general election we gave voice to those criticisms only internally rather than publicly, at meetings of the Parliamentary Party and in private representations to Ministers. But by mid-1946 we realised sadly that those procedures were getting us nowhere, and that, however reluctantly, we would have to go public if we wanted our views to be heard and considered. The way we chose to do that was to put down a critical amendment on the Address for the King's Speech inaugurating the 1946–47 Session. . . .

Mind you, we weren't hurling thunderbolts of condemnation at our leaders, much less rolling out the tumbrils to cart them off to Tyburn Gate. Our amendment, modest and moderate, was couched in terms of sweet reason. . . . You wouldn't think, would you, that this was calculated to shock-horror any member of a democratic socialist party. Moreover, Crossman, in moving the amendment, and those who spoke in support of him were at pains to pay tribute to the achievements of the Government . . . and to balance criticisms of United States policy with an attack on the ideology of one-party communism. . . . But we got little thanks for our moderation: both Attlee and Bevin were furious with us almost to the point of hysteria.

Ian Mikardo (**99**), pp. 99–103.

document 11
Independence for India

Rapidly changing circumstances were to upset the government's carefully controlled time-table for Indian independence.

It has long been the policy of successive British Governments to work towards the realization of self-government in India. In pursuance of this policy an increasing measure of responsibility has been devolved on Indians and today the civil administration and the Indian Armed Forces rely to a very large extent on Indian civilians and officers. . . . In 1940 the Coalition Government recognized the principle that Indians should themselves frame a new constitution for a fully autonomous India, and in the offer of 1942 they invited them to set up a Constituent Assembly for this purpose as soon as the war was over.

His Majesty's Government believe this policy to have been right and in accordance with sound democratic principles. Since they came into office, they have done their utmost to carry it forward to its fulfilment. The Cabinet Mission which was sent to India last year spent over three months in consultation with Indian leaders in order to help them to agree upon a method for determining the future constitution of India, so that the transfer of power might be smoothly and rapidly effected. . . . Since the return of the Mission an Interim Government has been set up at the centre composed of political leaders of the major communities exercising wide powers within the existing constitution. . . .

It is with great regret that His Majesty's Government find that there are still differences among Indian Parties which are preventing the Constituent Assembly from functioning as it was intended that it should. It is of the essence of the plan that the Assembly should be fully representative. His Majesty's Government desire to hand over their responsibility to authorities established by a constitution approved by all parties in India in accordance with the Cabinet Mission's plan, but unfortunately there is at present no clear prospect that such a constitution and such authorities will emerge. The present state of uncertainty is fraught with danger and cannot be indefinitely prolonged. His Majesty's Government wish to make it clear that it is their definite intention to take the necessary steps to effect the transference of power into responsible Indian hands by a date not later than June 1948.

Statement of Policy by United Kingdom Government, 20 February 1947: cited in N. Mansergh (ed.). *Documents and Speeches on British Commonwealth Affairs 1931–1952*, Volume II, Oxford University Press, 1953, pp. 659–61.

document 12

Bevin at the Foreign Office

Any criticisms of Ernest Bevin within the party were not shared by his staunchest supporter in Cabinet discussions on foreign policy, the Prime Minister.

'If you have a good dog don't bark yourself' is a good proverb and in Mr Bevin I had an exceptionally good dog. . . . The disturbed international situation was a constant anxiety during the whole of our period of office and the work of the Foreign Secretary was very exacting. Bevin knew his own mind, was a first-class negotiator and evoked loyal co-operation from all. He was very conscious always of the economic issues that underlay so many international questions and worked in close co-operation with successive Chancellors of the Exchequer.

Our policy was based on support for the United Nations Organisation and an honest endeavour to work in close harmony with the United States and with Soviet Russia. Unfortunately, we experienced opposition everywhere from the latter. . . . While this friction with Russia increased we naturally drew closer with the United States. This was helped by a change in the attitude of the Administration as they realised what the assumption of responsibility in world affairs entailed. The holding of the Secretaryship of State by General Marshall was an important factor in the promotion of good relations. It was Bevin who, by his quick follow-up of General Marshall's speech, made it a prime event. . . .

The making of the Brussels Treaty and of the Atlantic Pact, which was the work of Bevin, was a recognition of the fact that before Russia would consider reasonable relations with the free world there must be a building up of strength; strength was the only factor which the Russians considered.

Clement Attlee (**83**), pp. 196–7.

document 13
Consolidation and the 1950 election

The central theme of Labour's 1950 manifesto was 'consolidation' of past achievements; the emphasis and style was in clear contrast to 1945 [doc 1].

We ask our fellow citizens to assert in their free exercise of the franchise that by and large the first majority Labour Government has served the country well. The task now is to carry the nation through to complete recovery. And that will mean continued, mighty efforts from us all. The choice for the electors is between the Labour Party – the party of positive action, of constructive progress, the true party of the nation – and the Conservative Party – the party of outdated ideas, of unemployment, of privilege. . . .

No doubt there have been mistakes. But judge on what basis you will – by the standard of life of the general body of citizens, by employment, by the infrequency of serious industrial disputes, by the stability of the nation, by social security – by any fair comparison, the British people have done an infinitely better job than was done after the First World War. . . .

Our appeal is to all those useful men and women who actively contribute to the work of the nation. We appeal to manual workers – skilled, semi-skilled, and so-called unskilled; farmers and agricultural workers; active and able administrators in industry and the public services; professional workers, technicians and scientists; and housewives and women workers of all kinds. And just as we in this declaration have put the general public interest first, we ask the electors of all classes to do the same. For if they put sectional interests in front of the general good of the people as a whole, they will tend to damage, not only the nation, but themselves.

The fundamental question for the men and women of the United Kingdom to determine when they vote is this: Shall we continue along the road of ordered progress which the people deliberately chose in 1945, or shall reaction, the protectors of privilege and the apostles of scarcity economics be once more placed in the seats of power, to take us back to the bleak years of poverty and unemployment? Those years must never return.

We are successfully going forward with the great and inspiring adventure of our time. Let us win through together.

Let Us Win Through Together: A Declaration of Labour Policy for the Consideration of the Nation, 1950.

document 14

Cripps as Chancellor

Looking back from the vantage point of 1952, Robert Hall, who worked alongside Cripps as Director of the Economic Section of the Cabinet, summed up the record of the 'Cripps era'.

We have all been upset by Stafford Cripps' death. He was one of the great men of our time: I hardly knew Winston in the war, the greatest of them. I knew Keynes a bit and always thought he was the most distinguished brain in the country. But I worked closely with Stafford from late 1947 until he retired in 1950 and I thought he was in almost all respects an outstanding character. From the time Bevin began to break up until he retired, Stafford was by far the strongest and most respected man in the Cabinet. He commanded almost uncritical respect among senior civil servants, which is very unusual in my experience. He was a wonderful man to work for especially if he respected you: once he was convinced he made much more of one's arguments than one could oneself, and he was almost over-loyal to his subordinates: not only would he take their faults on himself but he tended to think more of them because he was defending them. This, like his advocacy of his brief, was partly due to his experience as a barrister. He did not really understand the basis of economic planning as we developed it under his regime, but he was entirely responsible for its development. It is true that Dalton introduced a deflationary Budget in November 1947 – the one Cripps took over – but it was not part of a plan and Dalton himself had done a good deal to stoke the fires of inflation. Cripps from the first thought that the problems should be treated as a whole, as is clear from the opening words of his own first Budget speech. . . .

His weakness was really his emotional belief in Socialism, which allowed Nye Bevan to defeat him on several crucial matters. In my view, it was the constant tendency of Government expenditure to rise which was the great handicap of the Government from 1946 to 1951 and Nye was the main force behind this, not only on health but on the extravagant housing and in his general pressure. Stafford would never stand up to him in the end and that was why Nye said that (in effect) he had out-manoeuvred him on several occasions. This was because Stafford's conscience was against him.

A. Cairncross (ed.) (**86**): diary entry, 29 April 1952, pp. 222–3.

document 15

Reaction to the 1950 result

*Unlike the euphoria that greeted news of the 1945 landslide [**doc. 2**], the narrowness of the victory in 1950 left senior Labour members with no illusions about the difficulty of the task ahead. The following extract is from Hugh Dalton's diary.*

Cabinet at 11. Attlee says we should carry on since we have a majority, even though a bare half dozen in new House. All present agree – Bevan, Tom Williams and Woodburn only absentees. . . . Most think – and I most emphatically – that this Parliament can't last more than a few months. But Bevin thinks we should stay in and 'consolidate'. . . . Cripps says cost of living is bound to rise and Budgetary position is very difficult. We all place our offices at PM's disposal, following custom after an election. Creech Jones, only defeated Cabinet Minister, made a great fight at Shipley, ruined by redistribution, and only lost by 81. . . .

Make note on situation, which seems very gloomy. Worst possible situation. If we had lost 10 seats more, Tories would have had bare majority, and would have had to form a powerless government; if we had lost 10 seats less we would have had a majority between 20 and 30 and could have scraped along for a bit. As it is, we have office without authority or power, and it is difficult to see how we can improve our position. So strong in mining and industrial centres and in big cities, and yet so weak in House of Commons. The rural areas, with few exceptions, very disappointing.

Unless we can create some new issue, favourable to ourselves, every week we stay in office (without authority and without a working majority, and with events moving against us – prices, cost of living, unpopular Budget etc.) we lose ground. Therefore we should either dissolve as soon as possible, or put the Tories in, letting them beat us on the Address, c.g. on steel. Some of our colleagues are still living in a world of illusion – as though the Opposition didn't exist, or had no brains.

B. Pimlott (ed.) (**102**): diary entries for 25–26 February 1950, pp. 470–1.

Health Service charges: Gaitskell's view

Writing shortly after Bevan's resignation, the Chancellor made the case that Health Service economies were necessary in both the national and party interest.

The events which I now record began as far as I am concerned with my earliest examination of how we should meet the budgetary problem this year. It was clear that we were bound to have to impose some additional taxation, and although I was not sure of the extent of this I reckoned that it might be to the order of £200 millions and would not be less than £100 millions. I felt that it was vital from the political angle that we should make a tremendous effort to economise on civil expenditure so that we could say to the country that only part of the burden was being carried by higher taxation. . . .

I had warned the PM that I felt extremely strongly about the necessity for some scheme of this kind, and had hinted at my resignation. . . .

The discussion [in Cabinet, March 1951] was not very exciting; the chief row occurring between Shinwell and Bevan when Bevan began to attack the arms programme in the middle of the discussion. The Cabinet of course were not aware at that time of the full Budget proposals. I could only say to them that there were going to be substantial increases in taxation, and I thought that [health] charges would not in themselves loom very large in the background of the other changes. At the end of the discussion when the voices had been collected Bevan said that it was no use his staying any longer and went a stage further in the threat to resign. . . .

On the Monday afternoon Bevan made his [resignation] statement in the House. . . . It was an extraordinary performance, totally lacking in any understanding of what people expected, and turned opinion even more sharply against him – on top of the *Tribune* article. The following day a special Party meeting took place. . . . Bevan made things even worse for himself by . . . a shocking outburst of bad temper which was evidently a revelation to many people in the Party. He almost screamed at the platform. At one point he said, 'I won't have it, I won't have it'. And, this of course was greeted with derision. '*You* won't have it?' called other Members of the Party. . . .

I have tried to tell this story baldly and without comment so that it may be of some value as a historical record. I permit myself now only two comments. First, that although I embarked on this with the knowledge that it would be a hard struggle I did not think it would be quite so tough. I suppose that if I had realised that there were so many things which could have meant defeat, I might never have begun; or at least I would have surrendered early on. . . .

The second observation is this. People of course are now beginning to look to the future. They expect that Bevan will try and organise the Constituency parties against us, and there may be a decisive struggle at the Party Conference in October. . . . He can exploit all the Opposition-mindedness which is so inherent in many Labour Party Members who having been agin so many Governments find it pretty hard work supporting even their own, especially when it does something unpopular.

All the same, with all the risks I think I was right. I said in the middle of one discussion to Hugh Dalton, 'It is really a fight for the soul of the Labour Party'. More people understand that this was so now. But who will win it? No one can say as yet. I am afraid that if Bevan does we shall be out of power for years and years.

P. Williams (ed.) (**108**): diary entry for 30 April 1951, pp. 239–57.

document 17
Health Service charges: Bevan's view

Edited by Jennie Lee and Michael Foot, Tribune *forcefully put the case for Bevan: that Health Service charges were only one unacceptable element of the Chancellor's Budget.*

'Now that sufficient time has passed to enable us to gather up general impressions and reactions to the Budget, we are in a better position to discuss it than immediately after the Chancellor of the Exchequer made his statement. I shall not say that the dominant feeling inspired by reflection is one of relief. . . . The sense of relief to which I have alluded is enhanced by the fact that probably few, if any, Budgets in recent years have been anticipated with so much anxiety.'

These sentiments have a contemporary flavour. They are, in fact, the opening passage in the speech of Mr Neville Chamberlain on behalf of the Tory opposition following Mr Phillip [*sic*] Snowden's Budget statement in April, 1931. A few months later the 1929–31 Labour Government collapsed. The City, the permanent officials at the Treasury, Mr Montagu Norman as Governor of the Bank of England had their way with poor Philip Snowden. . . .

We have had to wait 20 years for a Labour Chancellor to win
such warm approval in Conservative quarters. . . . Mr Gaitskell has
made the grade. And the reality should not be concealed because
many Labour Members, too, greeted the Budget with a sense of
enthusiastic relief. Now, as then, the majority of Labour MPs are
proud of their Chancellor, impressed by his mastery of intricate
financial matters and lulled into a false sense of security by their
certainty that he is a good man who would not willingly do them
wrong. The parallel might be too close for comfort. In that wretched
1929 Parliament, whose record no Socialist now defends, most
Labour Members were blind to Snowden's shortcomings. They allowed themselves to be led like lambs to the slaughter. Only when
it was too late did they look back to unravel the causes of their un-
doing.

In our view, therefore, the time to examine the potential economic
and political consequences of Mr Gaitskell is now. . . . Let us apply
the single Socialist test: has the Chancellor attempted to share fairly
the burdens of rearmament now being imposed on the nation?

A few days before the Budget the price of bread went up and the
pegging of food subsidies in the Budget means that we shall have to
face further increases in the price of essential foods in coming weeks
and months. . . . The cold fact is that rising prices are now cutting
the value of the social services and reducing the standard of life of
great numbers of our people. The Budget should have been used as
an instrument to mitigate the effects of these happenings for those
who are hurt most. Not merely has it done nothing of the kind; it
has attempted nothing of the kind.

Tribune, 20 April 1951.

document 18

Labour out of office, 1951

*Douglas Jay here sums up what he saw as the causes and consequences of
Labour's defeat in the 1951 election.*

It was the most fiercely fought, passionate, neck-and-neck, exhaust-
ing parliamentary election I ever contested (out of eleven). I also
cared more about the result of this election, together with 1950 and
1959, than any other, pushing myself again to the physical limit.
But the Labour Party had almost everything in 1951 against it: the
redistribution of seats, the Bevanite quarrel only six months before,

the loss of Bevin and Cripps, the Korean War burden, and the steady swing back of votes due to the revival of anti-Labour propaganda in the post-1945 press. Even on top of all this, the withdrawal of a large number of Liberal candidates, as compared with 1950, undoubtedly favoured the Conservatives. . . . In all the circumstances the result was as surprising as it was ironic. It was indeed a close-run thing. Labour won more votes than ever before, or since, more than the Conservatives, and more than any political Party ever had. But the Conservatives won more seats in the Commons. . . .

Yet the statistical accident of the 1951 result, by which the Party with the most votes failed to get the most seats, determined the course of British politics for more than twelve years afterwards. The Government that won in 1951 was destined to coast along into the economically easy years of 1952, 1953 and 1954, when, after the Korean war boom, the balance of trade fell back naturally in favour of this country, and we had the wit to continue the policy of buying food and materials from the world's most efficient producers. This made possible, thanks to the tough policies followed up till 1951, the first rise in real living standards since 1939 and a relaxation of controls and restrictions. That in turn was bound to gain support for whatever government was in power after 1952, as the Conservatives found in the elections of 1955 and 1959. Yet the chance to reap these rewards derived from the paradoxical 1951 result, and this result in turn stemmed from Cripps's refusal to allow the 1950 election to be postponed until after the April 1950 Budget. Had it been so postponed, it is highly probable that Labour would have won in 1950 by a rather larger margin, and Attlee would have felt no compulsion to call another election in 1951. In that case the post-war Labour Government would itself in all human probability have coasted through to the easy years.

Douglas Jay (**96**), pp. 210–14.

Glossary

atomic bombs   Intensive research during the Second World War provided the Americans with the first nuclear weapons, dropped with devastating effect on Hiroshima and Nagasaki in August 1945.

Beveridge Report   Report produced by Sir William Beveridge which proposed a unified scheme of social insurance. Labour incorporated the main proposals in the 1946 National Insurance Act.

Blitz   Attempt by the German Air Force to destroy civilian morale in Britain by systematic bombing of major cities, lasting for some nine months after September 1940.

Clause Four Socialism   Clause Four of Labour's constitution, adopted in 1918, committed the party to aim for 'the common ownership of the means of production, distribution and exchange'.

coalition government, 1940–45   Wartime administration formed under Winston Churchill in May 1940, containing representatives of the Conservative, Labour and Liberal Parties.

contracting out   In place of the system whereby individuals had to opt positively for payment of a trade-union levy to the Labour Party, Attlee's government legislated for a system under which union members either 'contracted out' or found a personal levy automatically going towards party funds.

demand management   The idea of government intervention in the economy to counteract cyclical depression and unemployment by maintaining aggregate demand.

Independent Labour Party   First founded in 1893, and concentrated in the industrial north of England and Scotland, it became a powerful force in the emerging Labour Party after 1900.

Industrial Charter   Major policy document produced by the Conservatives in opposition, accepting much of Labour's nationalisation programme and aiming to show that the party was attuned to the wishes of the electorate.

'Keep Left' group   Small group of Labour MPs, who emerged in 1947 with the aim of urging ministers to adopt a new foreign policy, independent of the United States and the Eastern Bloc.

Lend-Lease Programme of American economic aid, worth over 25 billion dollars, to Britain and its allies during the Second World War.

Mandate (Palestine) The peace conferences at the end of the First World War confirmed Britain's control, or mandate, in Palestine, which had been under British military rule since 1918.

Marshall Plan Informal name for the European recovery programme of 1948–51, financed by the United States and proposed by the Secretary of State, George Marshall.

mixed economy An economy containing a combination of both state-controlled and privately owned industries.

National government Conservative-dominated coalition first established in 1931 to tackle the national economic crisis; supported by MacDonald's 'National Labour' group but bitterly opposed by the official Labour opposition throughout the 1930s.

National Investment Council Established in 1946 to stimulate investment, especially in pre-war depressed areas.

NEC Labour's National Executive Committee, traditionally dominated by trade-union representatives, and charged with running the party between meetings of the annual conference.

neo-pacifism An emphasis on disarmament and the peaceful resolution of disputes through the League of Nations, favoured by many Labour supporters as the basis for British foreign policy.

physical control economic planning The notion that the British economy could only operate successfully if central government imposed a series of controls over production and consumption.

Potsdam Conference One of a series of peace conferences held at the end of the Second World War at which allied leaders defined the main outlines of a peace settlement.

Sterling area Bloc of countries tied by economic interests to the pound sterling; formed in 1931.

'Tito of Tonypandy' Term of abuse directed at the Welsh minister, Aneurin Bevan, comparing him with the ruthless Yugoslavian dictator.

Truman Doctrine Doctrine outlined by President Truman, under which the USA promised to support 'free people who are resisting subjugation', reflecting American hostility to Soviet Communism.

Wall Street crash With confidence in the American economy evaporating, share prices slumped and led to panic selling in October 1929. This crash sparked off a deep recession, with world unemployment doubling within a year.

Glossary

Western front The heaviest casualties of the First World War resulted from the prolonged military stalemate between German and allied forces in western Europe, who faced each other in trenches running from the English Channel to the Swiss frontier.

Bibliography

GENERAL POLITICAL

1   Addison, P., *The Road to 1945. British Politics and the Second World War*, Jonathan Cape, 1975.
2   Alderman, R. K., 'Discipline in the Parliamentary Labour Party, 1945–51', *Parliamentary Affairs*, xvii, 1965.
3   Brooke, S., 'Labour's War: Party, Coalition and Domestic Reconstruction, 1939–45', Oxford University D.Phil. thesis, 1988.
4   Butler, D. E., *The British General Election of 1951*, Macmillan, 1952.
5   Calder, A., *The People's War. Britain 1939–1945*, Jonathan Cape, 1969.
6   Cook, C. and Ramsden, J., eds., *By-Elections in British Politics*, Macmillan, 1973.
7   Eatwell, R., *The 1945–1951 Labour Governments*, Batsford, 1979.
8   Hennessy, P., *Whitehall*, Secker & Warburg, 1989.
9   Hennessy, P. and Seldon, A., eds., *Ruling Performance. British Governments from Attlee to Thatcher*, Basil Blackwell, 1987.
10 Hinton, J., *Labour and Socialism. A History of the British Labour Movement 1867–1974*, Wheatsheaf Books, 1983.
11 Hoffman, J. D., *The Conservative Party in Opposition 1945–51*, MacGibbon & Kee, 1964.
12 Howell, D., *British Social Democracy*, Croom Helm, 1976.
13 Jay, D., 'The Attlee Government', *Contemporary Record*, ii, iv, 1988.
14 Jefferys, K., *The Churchill Coalition and Wartime Politics 1940–1945*, Manchester University Press, 1991.
15 Laybourn, K., *The Rise of Labour. The British Labour Party 1890–1987*, Edward Arnold, 1988.
16 McCallum, R. B. and Readman, A., *The British General Election of 1945*, Oxford University Press, 1947.
17 McKibbin, R., *The Evolution of the Labour Party 1910–1924*, Oxford University Press, 1974.
18 Miliband, R., *Parliamentary Socialism*, Allen & Unwin, 1961.

19 Morgan, K. O., *Rebirth of a Nation: Wales 1880–1980*, Oxford University Press and University of Wales Press, 1981.

20 Morgan, K. O., *Labour in Power 1945–1951*, Oxford University Press, 1984.

21 Morgan, K. O., *Labour People. Leaders and Lieutenants, Hardie to Kinnock*, Oxford University Press, 1987.

22 Morgan, K. O., *The People's Peace. British History 1945–1989*, Oxford University Press, 1990.

23 Nicholas, H. G., *The British General Election of 1950*, Macmillan, 1951.

24 Pelling, H., *The Labour Governments, 1945–51*, Macmillan, 1984.

25 Pelling, H., 'The Labour Government of 1945–1951', in Bentley, M. and Stevenson, J., eds., *High and Low Politics in Modern Britain*, Oxford University Press, 1983.

26 Pimlott, B., *Labour and the Left in the 1930s*, Cambridge University Press, 1977.

27 Pritt, D. N., *The Labour Government 1945–51*, Lawrence & Wishart, 1963.

28 Ramsden J., '"A Party for Owners or a Party for Earners?" How Far did the British Conservative Party Really Change after 1945?' *Transactions of the Royal Historical Society*, 1987.

29 Rubinstein, D., 'Socialism and the Labour Party: the Labour Left and Domestic Policy 1945–1950', in Martin, D. E. and Rubinstein, D., eds., *Ideology and the Labour Movement*, Croom Helm, 1979.

30 Saville, J., *The Labour Movement in Britain*, Faber & Faber, 1988.

31 Schneer, J., *Labour's Conscience. The Labour Left 1945–51*, Unwin Hyman, 1988.

32 Sissons, M. and French, P., eds., *Age of Austerity 1945–51*, Penguin, 1964.

33 Skidelsky, R., *Politicians and the Slump. The Labour Government of 1929–31*, Macmillan, 1967.

34 Williams, P., 'Foot-faults in the Gaitskell–Bevan Match', *Political Studies*, xxvii, 1979.

35 Wood, J., 'The Labour Left in the Constituency Labour Parties, 1945–51', Warwick University MA thesis, 1977.

ECONOMIC AND SOCIAL POLICY

36 Alford, B. W. E., *British Economic Performance, 1945–1975*, Macmillan, 1988.

37 Addison, P., *Now the War is Over. A Social History of Britain 1945–51*, BBC and Jonathan Cape, 1985.

38 Barker, P., ed., *Founders of the Welfare State*, Heinemann, 1984.

39 Barker, R., *Education and Politics. A Study of the Labour Party 1900–1951*, Oxford University Press, 1972.

40 Barnett, C., *The Audit of War: The Illusion and Reality of Britain as a Great Power*, Macmillan, 1986.

41 Benn, C., 'Comprehensive School Reform and the 1945 Labour Government', *History Workshop*, x, 1980.

42 Booth, A., 'The Keynesian Revolution in Economic Policy-making', *Economic History Review*, xxxvi, 1983.

43 Brady, R. A., *Crisis in Britain*, Cambridge University Press, 1950.

44 Cairncross, A., ed., *Sir Richard Clarke. Anglo-American Co-operation in War and Peace, 1942–1949*, Oxford University Press, 1982.

45 Cairncross, A., *Years of Recovery. British Economic Policy 1945–51*, Methuen, 1985.

46 Chester, D. N., *The Nationalisation of British Industry 1945–51*, HMSO, 1975.

47 Deacon, A. and Bradshaw, J., *Reserved for the Poor: The Means Test in British Social Policy*, Robertson, 1983.

48 Dow, J. C. R., *The Management of the British Economy 1945–1960*, Cambridge University Press, 1964.

49 Gardner, R. N., *Sterling-Dollar Diplomacy*, McGraw-Hill, 1969.

50 Hess, J., 'The Social Policy of the Attlee Government', in Mommsen, W. J., ed., *The Emergence of the Welfare State in Britain and Germany*, Croom Helm, 1981.

51 Hughes, B., 'In defence of Ellen Wilkinson', *History Workshop*, vii, 1979.

52 Marwick, A., 'The Labour Party and the Welfare State in Britain 1900–1948', *American Historical Review*, lxxiii, 1967.

53 Merrett, S., *State Housing in Britain*, Routledge & Kegan Paul, 1979.

54 Middlemas, K., *Power, Competition and the State*, Vol. 1, *Britain in Search of Balance, 1940–61*, Macmillan, 1986.

55 Milward A. S., *The Reconstruction of Western Europe 1945–1951*, Methuen, 1984.

56 Panitch, L., *Social Democracy and Industrial Militancy: The Labour Party, the Trades Unions and Incomes Policy 1945–74*, Cambridge University Press, 1976.

57 Postan, M. M., *An Economic History of Western Europe 1945–64*, Methuen, 1967.
58 Robertson, A., *The Bleak Midwinter, 1947*, Manchester University Press, 1987.
59 Rogow, A. A. and Shore, P., *The Labour Government and British Industry, 1945–51*, Basil Blackwell, 1955.
60 Rollings, N., 'British Budgetary Policy 1945–1954: A "Keynesian Revolution"?' *Economic History Review*, xli, 1988.
61 Rubinstein, D., 'Ellen Wilkinson Reconsidered', *History Workshop*, vii, 1979.
62 Tomlinson, J., *Employment Policy: The Crucial Years 1939–55*, Oxford University Press, 1987.
63 Webster, C., *The Health Services since the War*, Vol. 1, *The National Health Service before 1957*, HMSO, 1988.

OVERSEAS POLICY
64 Anderson, T. H., *The United States, Great Britain and the Cold War 1944–1947*, University of Missouri Press, 1981.
65 Bartlett, C. J., *British Foreign Policy in the Twentieth Century*, Macmillan, 1989.
66 Bethell, N., *The Palestine Triangle: The Struggle between the British, the Jews and the Arabs, 1935–48*, Futura, 1980.
67 Darwin, J., *Britain and Decolonisation. The Retreat from Empire in the Post-War World*, Macmillan, 1988.
68 Dilks, D., ed., *Retreat from Power. Studies in Britain's Foreign Policy of the Twentieth Century*, Vol. 2, *After 1939*, Macmillan, 1981.
69 Dockrill, M., *British Defence since 1945*, Basil Blackwell, 1988.
70 Douglas, R., *World Crisis and British Decline, 1929–56*, Macmillan, 1986.
71 Gallagher, J., *The Decline, Revival and Fall of the British Empire*, Cambridge University Press, 1982.
72 Gowing, M. M. and Arnold L., *Independence and Deterrence: Britain and Atomic Energy, 1945–1952*, Macmillan, 1974.
73 Gupta, P. S., *Imperialism and the British Labour Movement, 1914–1964*, Holmes & Meier, 1975.
74 Hogan, M. J., *The Marshall Plan: America, Britain and the Reconstruction of Western Europe*, Cambridge University Press, 1987.
75 Jones, B. *The Russia Complex: The British Labour Party and the Soviet Union*, Manchester University Press, 1978.

76 Louis, W. R., *The British Empire in the Middle East, 1945–1951*, Oxford University Press, 1984.

77 Moore, R. J., *Escape from Empire*, Oxford University Press, 1983.

78 Newton, C. C. S., 'The Sterling Crisis of 1947 and the British Response to the Marshall Plan', *Economic History Review*, xxxi, 1984.

79 Ovendale, R., ed., *The Foreign Policy of the British Labour Governments, 1945–1951*, Leicester University Press, 1984.

80 Owen, N., 'Attlee Governments: The End of Empire 1945–51', *Contemporary Record*, iii, iv, 1990.

81 Pelling, H., *Britain and the Marshall Plan*, Macmillan, 1989.

82 Rothwell, V., *Britain and the Cold War 1941–1947*, Jonathan Cape, 1982.

BIOGRAPHIES, MEMOIRS AND DIARIES

83 Attlee, Clement, *As It Happened*, Heinemann, 1954.

84 Bullock, A., *The Life and Times of Ernest Bevin*, Vol. 3, *Foreign Secretary 1945–1951*, Heinemann, 1983.

85 Burridge, T., *Clement Attlee: A Political Biography*, Jonathan Cape, 1985.

86 Cairncross, A., ed., *The Robert Hall Diaries 1947–53*, Unwin Hyman, 1989.

87 Callaghan, James, *Time and Chance*, Collins, 1987.

88 Campbell, J., *Nye Bevan and the Mirage of British Socialism*, Weidenfeld & Nicolson, 1987.

89 Cooke, C., *The Life of Richard Stafford Cripps*, Hodder & Stoughton, 1957.

90 Dalton, Hugh, *High Tide and After: Memoirs 1945–60*, Muller, 1962.

91 Donoughue, B. and Jones, G. W., *Herbert Morrison: Portrait of a Politician*, Weidenfeld & Nicolson, 1973.

92 Foot, M., *Aneurin Bevan*, Vol. 2, *1945–1960*, Davis Poynter, 1973.

93 Griffiths, James, *Pages from Memory*, Dent, 1969.

94 Harris, J., *William Beveridge: A Biography*, Oxford University Press, 1977.

95 Harris, K., *Attlee*, Weidenfeld & Nicolson, 1982.

96 Jay, Douglas, *Change and Fortune: A Political Record*, Hutchinson, 1980.

97 Jefferys, K., ed., *Labour and the Wartime Coalition: From the Diary of James Chuter Ede 1941–1945*, The Historians' Press, 1988.

98 Lee, Jennie, *My Life with Nye*, Jonathan Cape, 1980.

99 Mikardo, Ian, *Back-Bencher*, Weidenfeld & Nicolson, 1988.

100 Morrison, H., *An Autobiography*, Odhams Press, 1960.

101 Pimlott, B., *Hugh Dalton*, Jonathan Cape, 1985.

102 Pimlott, B., ed., *The Political Diary of Hugh Dalton 1918–40, 1945–60*, Jonathan Cape, 1986.

103 Shinwell, Emanuel, *I've Lived Through It All*, Gollancz, 1973.

104 Vernon, B., *Ellen Wilkinson*, Croom Helm, 1982.

105 Wheeler-Bennett, J. W., *King George VI*, Macmillan, 1958.

106 Williams, F., *A Prime Minister Remembers. The War and Post-War Memoirs of Earl Attlee*, Heinemann, 1961.

107 Williams, P., *Hugh Gaitskell: A Political Biography*, Jonathan Cape, 1979.

108 Williams, P., ed., *The Diary of Hugh Gaitskell 1945–56*, Jonathan Cape, 1983.

Index